CAMBRIDGE
Lower Secondary
Global Perspectives

Noel Cassidy, Mike Gould, Mark Pedroz and Ed Walsh

Series Editor: Mark Pedroz

Stage 9: Student's Book

Published by Collins

An imprint of HarperCollins*Publishers*
The News Building, 1 London Bridge Street, London, SE1 9GF, UK

HarperCollins*Publishers*
Macken House, 39/40 Mayor Street Upper, Dublin 1, D01 C9W8, Ireland

Browse the complete Collins catalogue at
www.collins.co.uk

© HarperCollinsPublishers Limited 2023

10 9 8 7 6 5 4 3 2

ISBN 978-0-00-854940-4

British Library Cataloguing-in-Publication Data

A catalogue record for this publication is available from the British Library.

Series editor: Mark Pedroz
Authors: Noel Cassidy, Mike Gould, Mark Pedroz and Ed Walsh
Publisher: Elaine Higgleton
Product manager: Catherine Martin
Product developer: Saaleh Patel
Project manager and development editor: Caroline Low
Copy editor: Susan Ross, Ross Economics and Editorial Services Ltd
Proofreader: Claire Throp
Cover designer: Gordon McGilp
Cover image: Ann Paganuzzi
Internal designer: Ken Vail Graphic Design
Typesetter: David Jimenez
Production controller: Lyndsey Rogers
Printed and bound in India by Replika Press Pvt. Ltd.

Contents

Introduction: How to use this book   **v**

Chapter 1: Developing research methods and collaboration skills   **1**

1.1 Constructing research questions and locating information to answer them   2

1.2 Testing predictions and answering questions   6

1.3 Selecting and organising information   10

1.4 Working as a team to achieve a shared outcome   14

1.5 Applying what you have learned   18

Chapter 2: Improving analysis and evaluation   **23**

2.1 Identifying perspectives and synthesising arguments   24

2.2 Understanding the causes and consequences of a global issue   28

2.3 Evaluating sources for their credibility   32

2.4 Evaluating the structure and evidence in an argument   36

2.5 Conducting research and using it in arguments   40

2.6 Applying what you have learned   44

Chapter 3: Solving problems, suggesting outcomes   **49**

3.1 Working as a team to achieve a shared goal   50

3.2 Discussing information and developing understanding   54

3.3 Recommending action to address an issue   58

3.4 Reflecting on how a team can improve and succeed   62

3.5 Explaining how exploring different perspectives changes minds   66

3.6 Applying what you have learned   70

Chapter 4: Communicating ideas: improving your writing skills   **75**

4.1 Using and presenting research findings   76

4.2 Explaining causes and consequences   80

4.3 Explaining the strengths and weaknesses of arguments   84

4.4 Evaluating and referencing sources and evidence   88

4.5 Proposing a course of action   92

4.6 Applying what you have learned   96

4.7 Giving a personal response   100

Chapter 5: Planning and writing your research report 105

5.1 Exploring a range of relevant research questions and identifying the best one for you 106

5.2 Identifying a range of different sources to locate relevant information 110

5.3 Identifying and linking different perspectives, exploring causes and consequences 114

5.4 Selecting research methods to answer your question 118

5.5 Organising your findings and planning your research writing 122

5.6 Writing up your report with an introductory analysis of the issue 126

5.7 Developing your argument by evaluating different perspectives 130

5.8 Making a recommendation for action 134

5.9 Proofreading, checking and referencing your final report 138

5.10 Providing a critical bibliography 140

5.11 Explaining how your personal perspective has changed as a result of research 142

5.12 Reflecting on skills development and targets for improvement 144

Glossary of key terms 149

Acknowledgements 150

Introduction: How to use this book

The Collins Stage 9 Student's Book offers an introduction to Cambridge Global Perspectives™ at Lower Secondary level, with rich international texts, data and case studies to stimulate your thinking about contemporary global topics.

The book is organised into five chapters. Each chapter explores different issues and perspectives that are relevant to one or sometimes two of the syllabus topics. In Stage 9, the topics you will explore are 'Health and wellbeing', 'Poverty and inequality', 'Media and communication', 'Transport, travel and tourism', 'Sport and recreation', 'Climate change, energy and resources' and 'Water, food and agriculture'.

Chapter 1 focuses on developing your *research* skills and ability to *collaborate* as a group. You will research the relationship between poverty, wealth and disease, beginning with the historical example of TB and thinking about how countries can reduce the spread of infectious diseases in the future.

In Chapter 2, you will be deepening your *analysis* and *evaluation* skills, beginning to synthesise different arguments and perspectives, and evaluating longer, more complex sources, as you explore the issue of mobile phone use in school.

Chapter 3 will help you to *analyse* a situation and different possible solutions, *collaborating* as a team to explore these options and reaching agreement as a group on which one will work best. You will finish by *reflecting* on how your own view has developed through analysing and evaluating different perspectives and on how your teamwork could be improved.

In Chapter 4, you will focus on your *communication* skills, and especially on your writing skills to present research findings, explain causes and consequences, evaluate the strengths and weaknesses of arguments and the credibility of sources and to propose a course of action.

Chapters 1–4 each build to a final task that gives you the opportunity to draw together and apply your learning, as you investigate an issue from the chapter in more depth.

Finally, Chapter 5 allows you and your teachers to assess your progress, as you draw together your understanding from earlier chapters to undertake an individual research project. You will be supported to choose a topic, issue and question that interest you, and you will be guided through the process of researching and then writing a report. Examples of work, written by our authors, will be provided throughout for you to assess and learn from.

We hope our resources will support you to build skills that you can use in all the subjects you study at Lower Secondary. We hope, too, that the sources you encounter in the book will inspire you to investigate other global issues – the issues that are most important to you, your school, your culture, your local environment and the nation(s) to which you belong.

Mark Pedroz, Series Editor

Key features of the Student's Book

The **opening page** of each chapter summarises the skills, topic and issues to be explored, as well as the final task.

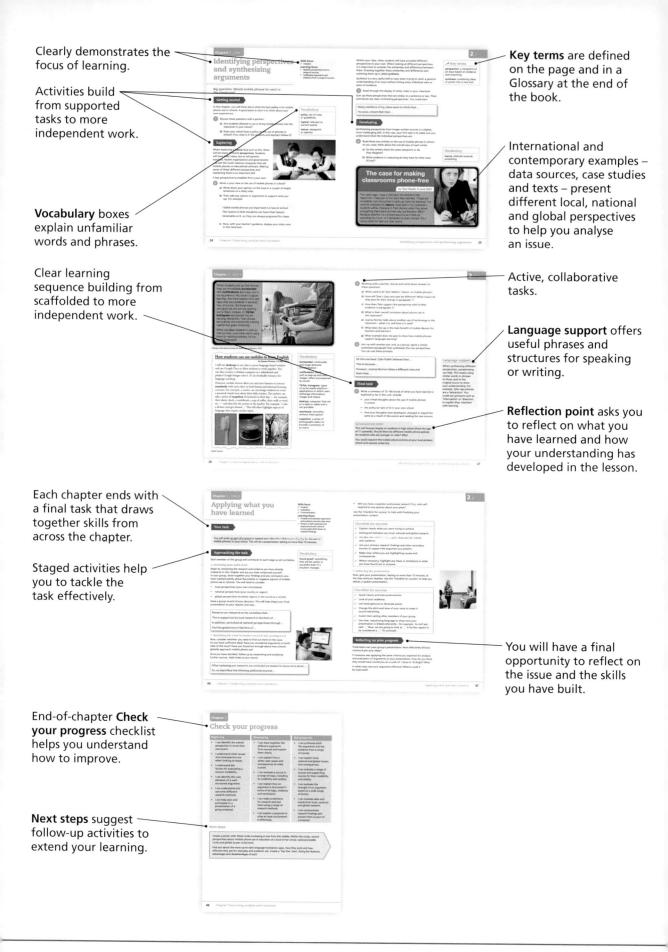

Clearly demonstrates the focus of learning.

Activities build from supported tasks to more independent work.

Vocabulary boxes explain unfamiliar words and phrases.

Clear learning sequence building from scaffolded to more independent work.

Each chapter ends with a final task that draws together skills from across the chapter.

Staged activities help you to tackle the task effectively.

End-of-chapter **Check your progress** checklist helps you understand how to improve.

Next steps suggest follow-up activities to extend your learning.

Key terms are defined on the page and in a Glossary at the end of the book.

International and contemporary examples – data sources, case studies and texts – present different local, national and global perspectives to help you analyse an issue.

Active, collaborative tasks.

Language support offers useful phrases and structures for speaking or writing.

Reflection point asks you to reflect on what you have learned and how your understanding has developed in the lesson.

You will have a final opportunity to reflect on the issue and the skills you have built.

Developing research methods and collaboration skills

1

Poverty and disease

Poverty and disease have often gone hand in hand – why is this? Does living in poverty mean you are more likely to become ill? Does being wealthy increase your chances of good health? In this chapter, you will find out about some of the links between poverty and disease, focusing on a disease called Tuberculosis (or TB). You will research inequality and health as both a national and a global issue.

In this chapter, you will explore the topics of 'Health and wellbeing' and 'Poverty and inequality', thinking about the following issues:

- **How are diseases linked to poverty?**
- **What does data show about the links between wealth and health?**
- **Is TB a problem with a solution?**
- **How can literacy help in the fight against TB?**

You will be developing a range of collaboration and research skills:

1.1 Constructing research questions and locating information to answer them

1.2 Testing predictions and answering questions

1.3 Selecting and organising information

1.4 Working as a team to achieve a shared outcome

1.5 Applying what you have learned.

Your final task will be to use ideas you have developed over the chapter to suggest lessons learned from research into major diseases. Some of these lessons will be applicable internationally, but there will also be consequences for national and local actions.

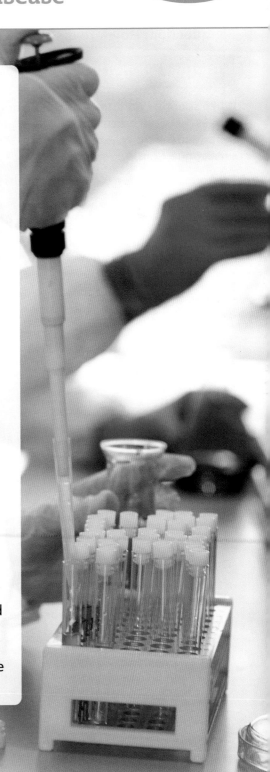

Constructing research questions and locating information to answer them

Skills focus
✓ Research

Learning focus
- Locate information to answer research questions.
- Reference source information accurately.

Big question: How are diseases linked to poverty?

Getting started

When scientists want to answer a big question such as 'How can we cure this disease?', they need to break the question down into several smaller questions. For example:

The common cold is a **viral infectious disease** that occurs all over the world.

How can we cure this disease?

How does someone catch this disease?

How does this disease spread?

How can we cure people who have caught it?

How can we stop this disease spreading?

1 **a)** In a table, record the four smaller questions on the right in the left column. In the right column, next to each question, suggest an answer in relation to the common cold. Draw on your own ideas and experiences.

b) Now suggest how you came up with those answers. How did you know? Make notes, then discuss them with a partner.

Exploring

When scientists conduct research, they ask questions and gather evidence. They find out what is already known and consider how new ideas challenge or support existing thinking.

Tuberculosis, often shortened to TB, has been around for thousands of years; at one point it was one of the most rampant illnesses in the world, killing thousands of people every year. It is still a serious infection.

2 Working with a partner, carry out a brief fact-finding mission on TB.

a) Using the internet or library resources, research:

- what TB is, its **symptoms** and how it spreads

- a brief history of the disease – when was it first identified, and how the number of cases of TB have changed globally in the last 100 years.

Vocabulary

viral: caused by a virus

infectious disease: illness caused by a micro-organism which can spread from person to person

symptom: any indication or characteristic sign of a disease

proximity: close together

b) Summarise your findings in a spider diagram.

c) Keep a record of all the sources you draw on.

A key idea we are going to explore in this chapter is the link between poverty and disease.

3 Working in a small group, discuss what you have found out about the causes of TB and consider which are linked to poverty. Record your ideas, making sure the links with poverty are clear. For example:

> The data show that the transmission of TB is more likely if people are living in close **proximity**. If people are poor, they are more likely to be forced to live in smaller and less well-ventilated homes, which will help TB to spread.

4 In your group, choose one aspect of TB and poverty that you want to research further. Then, decide on a suitable research question for that area of focus. Use the 'Checklist for success' to help you write good research questions.

Checklist for success

A good research question should:

✔ be written in plain English, using as few words as possible

✔ be based on a broad topic area but focused on a specific issue

✔ raise a problem to which there is a possible solution

✔ be something you can research information about

✔ be something it is possible to have different views on

✔ focus on an issue of importance to your own country – or a country you are familiar with.

Referencing sources

If the source is in book format, give the author's name (surname first), book or journal title (in *italics*), publisher and year of publication. For example:

- Henry, George. *Progress and Poverty*, Robert Schalkenbach Foundation, 2006.

If the source is a website, give the author's name, article title, website name, date of publication and URL. For example:

- Zaman, K. 'Tuberculosis: A Global Health Problem', *Bangladesh Journals Online*, April 2010, https://doi.org/10.3329/jhpn.v28i2.4879.

When noting down your ideas, you could:

- produce a list of bullet points

- draw a spider diagram or a flow diagram

- rank order the possible causes.

5 Share your group's research question with other groups. For example, you could display it on the board, or write it on a poster with space for feedback underneath.

a) Make comments on other groups' research questions – keep the comments positive and focus them on what is effective and how you think the question could be improved.

b) Review the feedback on your research question. Use it to help revise your research question, to improve it if needed.

Developing

The sample answers below summarise the development of a research question and the research into poverty and TB. A teacher has commented on sample answer A.

Sample answer A:

> My research question is 'Does poor housing make catching TB more likely?' I found an article that says that poor housing does make it more likely that you will catch TB because if housing is sub-standard, it is likely to be dark, poorly ventilated and overcrowded. If people are living in these conditions, it will be more likely that they will catch TB as it is a bacterium and spreads in the air. If people are poorer, it is more likely they will be in poor housing and so poverty does lead to TB.

Identifies nature of TB and links with housing conditions; explains why there may be a link. Uses just one unidentified source. No data provided to support arguments.

Sample answer B:

> My research question is 'Are people in crowded housing more likely to catch TB?' We found several studies; the most useful one was published in Hong Kong in 2013. This looked at 1787 cases and found not only that most were from a densely populated part of Kowloon but also that more cases came from lower down in tower blocks and fewer from higher up. This supports the idea that cramped housing with poor ventilation makes TB more likely.

6 Working on your own:

a) Which answer is stronger: A or B? Note down your reasons.

b) Write a tutor response to sample answer B.

7 Return to your group and your chosen research question on poverty and TB.

a) Carry out research to answer your research question. Keep detailed notes of all the sources you use.

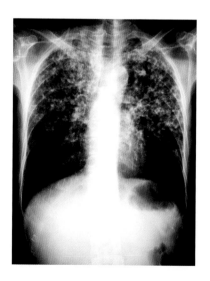

b) Briefly summarise your findings in two or three sentences.

c) Rank order the sources you used to show how useful they were in helping you answer your research question. Use the 'Checklist for success' to help you.

Checklist for success

Credible sources are generally:

✔ published on credible news websites   ✔ peer-reviewed

✔ academic publications and journals   ✔ based on facts

✔ fact-checked   ✔ based on arguments, not assertions.

---

d) Make notes on how much information you came across that was irrelevant and how you filtered this out.

e) Revisit your research question. Could it have been worded better? Make notes to explain your thinking.

Final task

8 Write a report on the findings of your group's research into TB and poverty. Your report should include a description of the process of research, including:

a) how you decided on your research question, and how you developed and refined it

b) a summary of your research findings

c) a list of the sources drawn on and how well you were able to use them

d) whether, on reflection, your research question could have been improved.

9 a) Present your findings as a group and then listen to the other groups' presentations. During each presentation, make notes on:

- how clear the research question was

- how well the group answered their research question

- the strength of sources referenced – were they relevant, reliable and well recorded?

b) Listen to the feedback on your group's presentation and then share your feedback with the other groups.

❓ REFLECTION POINT

Diseases are often global, spreading from country to country. Suggest why solutions to disease may have to be tailored to national or even local contexts.

Testing predictions and answering questions

Big question: What does data show about the links between wealth and health?

Getting started

1 Look at Figure 1.2.1.

In the graph:

• The red line shows how ice cream sales in a country in the **Northern Hemisphere** vary by month over the course of a year.

• The green line shows how, in the same country, the number of shark attacks vary during the year.

As you can see, the two lines are close together.

Note down your responses to these questions, then discuss answers in a group.

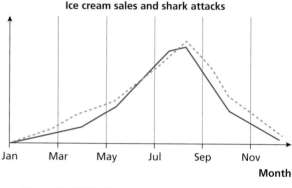

Figure 1.2.1: Ice cream sales and shark attacks.

a) What time of year are ice cream sales at their highest?

b) When are shark attacks most likely?

c) At what time of year are the lowest levels for these two **variables**?

d) What does this suggest about the relationship between ice cream sales and shark attacks?

2 Now look at Figure 1.2.2, which shows the estimated world pirate population plotted against the average global temperature.

> **Vocabulary**
>
> **Northern Hemisphere**: the northern half of the Earth (north of the equator)

> 🔑 **Key term**
>
> **variable**: characteristic, factor or quantity that can increase or decrease

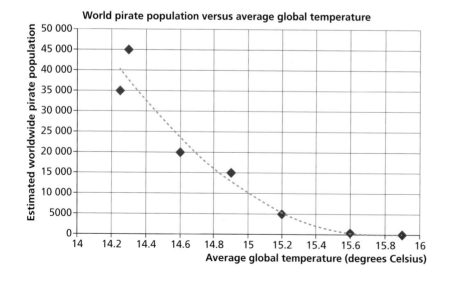

Figure 1.2.2: Pirates versus global temperature.

a) Suggest whether there is a good **correlation**.

b) Suggest whether there is **causation**.

c) Describe how you answered questions a and b.

d) Explain why establishing correlation is a different process to identifying a **causal link**.

> ### Exploring

If two sets of measurements rise and fall together, does this mean one thing causes the other?

In Figure 1.2.1, the **trends** are close, so the correlation is strong. However, this doesn't prove that an increase in shark attacks causes more ice creams to be sold or that selling more ice creams makes sharks attacks more likely.

So, are the two sets of figures simply coincidental? The data comes from a location where temperatures are highest in July and August. When it is hotter, people are more likely to buy ice cream and they are also more likely to go swimming in the sea, which means they are also more likely to be attacked by a shark. In other words, there is a *relationship* – but there is a third factor (seasonal temperature variation) that is driving both ice cream sales and shark attacks. So, the graph doesn't prove causation – it simply suggests a strong correlation.

3 A friend looks at Figure 1.2.2 and says, 'Well, at least something good will come out of global warming – there won't be as many pirates around!'

  a) Working with a partner, decide how you will respond to this comment.

  b) Join with another pair and discuss a good way of countering your friend's interpretation. Share your ideas with the class.

An advert claims that eating chocolate is a great cure for the common cold. The advert draws on the following research to make this claim: 159 people suffering from a common cold were given a bar of chocolate to eat each day; within a week, 76 per cent of them no longer had a cold.

4 In a small group:

  a) Suggest the problem with this research.

  b) Suggest how the research would benefit from a **control group**.

  c) Predict what a control group might have shown about the relationship between eating chocolate and no longer having a cold.

> ### 🔑 Key terms
>
> **correlation**: relationship between two variables
>
> **causation**: when one thing causes another
>
> **causal link**: a relationship based on causation
>
> **trend**: a general development in the way something happens; a pattern in data
>
> **control group**: research group that is not exposed to the experimental factor being tested, in this case eating chocolate

Developing

Let's now consider whether being wealthier means a person is less likely to die from TB.

Research carried out into the incidence of TB in India established several factors that have a strong correlation with TB:

A   Using tobacco

B   Exposure to indoor air pollution

C   Low **Body Mass Index (BMI)**

D   Daily alcohol use

E   **HIV**

F   **Diabetes.**

The researchers then explored how these factors correlated with levels of wealth. They found:

- The wealthiest in society had the lowest incidence in five of these factors.

- The poorest in society had the highest incidence in four of these factors.

In Figure 1.2.3, charts A–F summarise the research findings.

Figure 1.2.3: Prevalence of key TB risk factors (and 95% confidence interval) by wealth level.

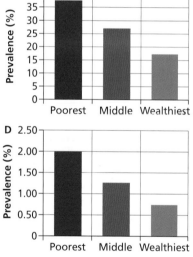
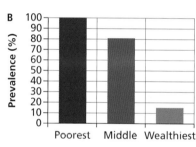
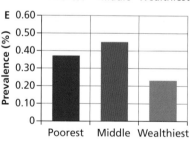
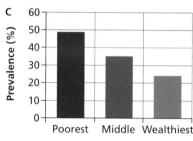
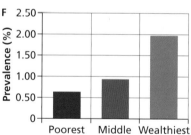

Source: Olivia Oxlade and Megan Murray, 'Tuberculosis and poverty: why are the poor at greater risk in India?', November 2019, National Library of Medicine.

5   Working on your own, note down your responses to these questions:

   a) What do these findings appear to suggest about the causal links between poverty and TB?

   b) Why should you be cautious about making any conclusions from the data at this stage?

6   Now, taking each chart A–F in turn, write a one-line summary of what the data show. For example, for C you could write: 'This chart shows that the wealthier people are, the less likely they are to be underweight.'

> **Vocabulary**
>
> **Body Mass Index (BMI)**: measure relating a person's mass to their height; a low BMI indicates a person is underweight
>
> **HIV**: Human Immunodeficiency Virus; a disease that attacks the body's immune system
>
> **diabetes**: medical condition resulting in high blood sugar levels, which causes a range of health problems

7 Again drawing on the data in the six charts:

a) Describe a person who is least likely to contract TB.

b) Describe a person who is most likely to contract TB.

c) Suggest why being wealthier makes it less likely you will contract TB.

d) Comment on the assertion 'Living in poverty increases your chances of having TB'.

Based on the research findings, the researchers decided to check the correlation between wealth and TB directly. Figure 1.2.4 is based on dividing the population of India according to wealth into five equal-sized groups (quintiles).

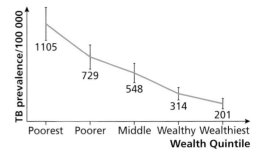

Figure 1.2.4: TB prevalence (per 100 000) by wealth quintile.

Source: Olivia Oxlade and Megan Murray, 'Tuberculosis and poverty: why are the poor at greater risk in India?', November 2019, National Library of Medicine.

8 Working on your own:

a) Suggest a conclusion you could draw from Figure 1.2.4.

b) Suggest whether the research data overall (Figures 1.2.3 and 1.2.4) establishes a causal link between poverty and the likelihood of contracting TB. Explain your reasoning.

Final task

When researching the links between poverty and TB in India, the researchers:

- identified variables, such as use of tobacco, that seemed to correlate with a higher incidence of TB

- researched the correlation of these variables with wealth

- checked the correlation directly between wealth and TB

- identified several areas that people and services could address to reduce the likelihood of contracting TB.

9 a) You will now work as a group to research data on disease and wealth:

- for a disease of your choice

- for a country of your choice.

b) Summarise your findings in a short presentation.

Draw on the India TB study and the 'Checklist for success' to guide your research and structure your presentation.

Checklist for success

✔ Draw on graphical data from a verified and reputable source.

✔ Display the data appropriately using charts, tables or graphs.

✔ Give a clear interpretation of the data to support the case being made.

✔ Explain any correlations identified.

✔ Finish with a conclusion that summarises the links between wealth and disease.

? REFLECTION POINT

Graph F (Figure 1.2.3) suggests that people who are wealthier are at greater risk of diabetes.

- Research diabetes and suggest why this might be the case.

- Suggest other ways in which being wealthier may increase your risk of disease.

Selecting and organising information

Big question: Is TB a problem with a solution?

Getting started

In 19th-century Britain, there was a widely held view that diseases were caused by foul smells (miasma). Because of this view, many people campaigned for cleaner towns and cities, including the proper disposal of **sewage** and rubbish. In fact, bad smells – while unpleasant – do not cause disease. Nevertheless, the cleaning up of towns and cities from the 1850s resulted in a noticeable drop in the incidence of infectious diseases, such as TB and cholera.

Working in pairs, answer these questions; be prepared to share your ideas with the rest of the class.

1 Suggest why an incorrect theory of disease **transmission** nevertheless produced a significant reduction in the **mortality rate**.

2 Figure 1.3.1 shows how the TB mortality rate in Britain altered between 1860 and 1950. Figure 1.3.2 shows recent data on the causes of TB. Use evidence from both sources to suggest why the generally downwards trend in mortality rate in Figure 1.3.1 shows two upturns.

> **Vocabulary**
>
> **sewage**: wastewater and human excrement
>
> **transmission**: the process of causing something to move from one place to another; here, disease spreading from one person to another
>
> **mortality rate**: the number of deaths in a given population within a defined period, usually a year

Figure 1.3.1: TB mortality rate in Britain, 1860–1950.

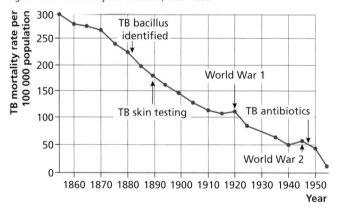

Source: Boston University School of Public Health.

Figure 1.3.2: Reasons for people falling ill with TB in 2021.

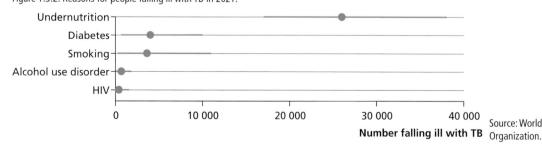

Source: World Health Organization.

Exploring

Vaccination has been an important tool in the fight against many types of infectious diseases for decades. Countries affected by the outbreak of an illness will be keen to source a vaccine that offers a degree of protection, or to develop a vaccine if none exists.

However, the use of a vaccine depends upon acceptance by the population. In some countries there is a very wide uptake of vaccines, while in other countries significant numbers of people prefer not to be vaccinated. In most countries it is still a matter of personal choice. However, this is not universal; some countries require people to be vaccinated against identified diseases in order to be able to enter the country or visit certain venues or to do certain jobs.

For this next activity you will work in a group to research attitudes towards vaccinations in your country – or a country of your choice.

3 In your group, discuss how you can find out about attitudes towards vaccination in your chosen country. For example, you could look at:

- data for vaccination rates

- articles about participation rates in vaccination programmes

- historical events linked to vaccination programmes

- the legal requirements for people to be vaccinated – for example, is **bodily autonomy** established in law, or is vaccination a legal requirement of entry or for working in certain job roles (for example, in health services)?

Organise your group to carry out the research.

4 Now, organise your research findings into a poster that summarises the overall national situation regarding vaccination in your chosen country. Think about how you could use **infographics** to summarise the data.

5 Next, join up with another group and consider the research methods you used to identify attitudes to vaccination in your chosen country.

a) Compare the research methods used.

b) Explain to the other group why your group used these methods and how well they worked.

c) Review each other's posters against these criteria:

- Gather relevant information from a wide range of sources.

- Organise research findings to present a clear and well-evidenced case.

- Justify the research method selected.

Discuss what worked well and what could be done differently next time. Agree recommendations for future research.

> ### Vocabulary
>
> **bodily autonomy**: the idea that each individual has the right to decide what is done to their body

> ### 🔑 Key term
>
> **infographic**: information displayed in an interesting way visually

Developing

For some years, there has been a vaccine (called the BCG vaccine) which can be used to protect people against TB. However, as with all vaccines, it is not 100 per cent effective. It works well with children but less so with adults.

6 Working with a partner:

a) Research the BCG vaccine and how effective it has been globally.

b) Based on your research findings, in which circumstances would you recommend the BCG vaccine? Summarise your findings in note form.

Refer to the 'Checklist for success' to support your research, selection and organisation of data.

Checklist for success

✔ Gather relevant information from a range of sources.

✔ Keep a clear record of the sources used.

✔ Organise your research findings to present a clear and well-evidenced case.

Some students have been set the following task, based on the above research:

> The health authorities in your country are concerned that the incidence of TB has risen sharply in the last few years. Using ideas from your research and working with a partner, write a blog post of around 100 words on how the authorities should react. The piece should clearly indicate what course of action you are recommending and why.

7 Working on your own:

a) Compare sample answer B with sample answer A. Which is the stronger answer and why?

b) Write a teacher comment on sample answer B.

Sample answer A:

The government should watch the trends in data but not immediately intervene. The BCG vaccine is less than 100 per cent effective and noticeably less effective in adults than in children. Of children vaccinated, 20 per cent will not become infected and of those who do, it stops around half of them from getting the disease. I got this information from Wikipedia. Setting up a large-scale vaccination programme will be expensive, cause concern and will not be a total cure.

Relevant information is identified, recorded and presented in a logical way. The student recognises the effect of the vaccine varies globally. However, only one source is used. The student has not explored how to respond to the rising level of concern.

Sample answer B:

> The BCG vaccine is a useful tool in the fight against TB and should be used with children straightaway. According to WHO data, this will result in 20 per cent of children not becoming infected with TB. The WHO regards it as an essential medicine and an analysis of research projects indicates it halves the risk of getting TB.

Final task

8 Working on your own, write a 100–150-word response to the big question for this unit: 'Is TB a problem with a solution?'

Use the 'Checklist for success' to help you.

Checklist for success

- ✔ Give a clear indication of your answer to the question.
- ✔ Draw on various ideas from across the unit.
- ✔ Gather relevant information from a range of sources, including your own research.
- ✔ Conduct any additional research you feel is necessary.
- ✔ Indicate the sources you have used.
- ✔ Discuss the method you have used and justify it as a good way of exploring answers to the question.
- ✔ Present a clear and well-evidenced case.

❓ REFLECTION POINT

Reflect on how easy it is to gather the evidence you need to answer questions.

- Were there some types of evidence you wanted to use but could not locate?
- Suggest why some types of evidence are not so easy to access.

Working as a team to achieve a shared outcome

Skills focus
✓ Collaboration

Learning focus
- Collaborate with others effectively as part of a team.
- Use a variety of skills to make teamwork more effective.
- Contribute ideas and support others to achieve a shared outcome.

Big question: How can literacy help in the fight against TB?

World Health Organization poster to promote World Blood Donor Day, 2022.

Getting started

You have seen how education plays an important role in preventing the spread of disease.

1. Working on your own, consider your response to these questions, then share your views with a partner. Be ready to explain your thinking to the class.

   a) What can people learn about to help reduce the spread of disease?

   b) Do you think people who are more **literate** are better equipped to avoid contracting diseases such as TB? Why?

   c) How is the impact of education on disease transmission limited?

Exploring

Providing information and developing understanding are crucial in limiting the spread of infectious diseases. **Literacy rates** are therefore an important factor when considering how to communicate **public health programmes**.

This poster was produced by the World Health Organization (WHO) for World Blood Donor Day. It is an example of a public health campaign.

2. Work with a partner to examine the poster. Discuss:

   a) What are the key messages of the poster?

   b) How does the poster give this message?

   c) How successful do you think the poster is in achieving its aims as a public health campaign?

Vocabulary

literate: able to read and write

literacy rate: the proportion of the population of a certain age who can read and write

public health programme: government information campaign intended to prevent illness and disease transmission among the wider population; these may be general or targeted at specific risk groups

3 You will now work in a group to research and evaluate public health campaigns aimed at children or young people. You will need to look at several examples of campaigns, including those from your own country and abroad.

Within your group, you will need to agree:

- the key features to focus on when looking at each health campaign; this will ensure you can discuss similar features

- who is going to focus on which campaigns (for example, from which country)

- timings for the discussion, research and feedback.

4 Having carried out the research, discuss what makes a public health campaign effective. Use the 'Checklist for success' to support you in the group discussion.

Checklist for success

✔ Share knowledge of the campaigns studied.

✔ Agree on key strengths and weaknesses of the campaigns.

✔ Summarise the key features of effective campaigns, indicating what worked well and what was less effective.

✔ Arrive at a set of preferred criteria.

✔ Agree key guidelines for creating your own public health campaign aimed at 11-year-olds.

---

5 Now, consider your team-working process through the task. As a group, reflect and make notes on how well the group members worked together and identify any areas for improvement.

Developing

6 You will now work as part of a team to develop your own health education campaign targeted at 11-year-old students. The campaign will focus on how microbial diseases spread and what students can do to reduce disease transmission.

You will need to create a resource that a teacher can use for this purpose; this could be a leaflet, a slide presentation or a short video.

It is important that your campaign makes the following points clear:

- There are a range of infectious diseases that exist as **microbes**.

- Although microbes vary in terms of the effect they have on people, they all go through the same six stages of infection.

- How microbial infections affect the body during each of these six stages.

- What students can do to keep themselves safe.

> **Vocabulary**
>
> **microbe:** micro-organism (that is, an organism that can be seen only via a microscope), especially one that causes disease

You could use a table like the one below to record the key ideas your team is going to communicate about the six stages of disease infection. Or you could choose a planning format of your own.

Stage	What the microbes are doing at this stage in the process	What people can do to limit the effectiveness of the disease
1. Enter the body		
2. Colonise		
3. Persist		
4. Replicate		
5. Exit the body		
6. Evolve		

Refer to the 'Checklist for success' to help you organise your campaign and develop your collaboration skills.

Checklist for success

Organising your health education campaign:

✔ Select an infectious disease that is active in your area.

✔ Communicate key information about how this disease spreads in an age-appropriate way.

✔ Give practical and realistic health strategies that 11-year-olds can adopt in response to the disease.

Developing your collaboration skills:

✔ Cooperate well within your team to complete the campaign, for example by agreeing and sharing out tasks.

✔ Aim to develop your team-working skills, for example by contributing useful ideas, supporting other team members and helping to resolve disagreements.

7 Look at this sample answer to question 6. Decide how well it succeeds in the task for the target age group. Structure your comments using the headings 'What works well' and 'Even better if…'.

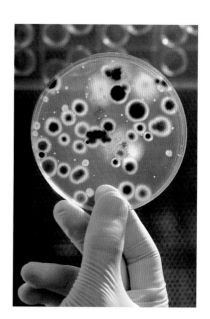

Some diseases are caused by bacterial infections. Bacteria can reproduce extremely quickly; to do so they grow, copy their DNA and then split into two daughter cells. Although this happens very quickly, it also means that all the bacteria are exact copies of each other. Therefore, only one drug is needed to treat a bacterial infection as it will attack all of the bacteria. However, some types of bacteria are now becoming drug resistant through mutation.

8 Now, review your group's ideas for a health education campaign for 11-year-olds on preventing disease transmission. Consider whether the content is appropriate for the age group. How could you test this out? For example, some members of the group may have younger siblings that the materials could be shown to, or there may be younger students in your school you could get reactions from.

Final task

9 Each group now needs to present its health education campaign for 11-year-olds on preventing disease transmission. In the case of a leaflet, copies can be handed to other groups; videos and presentations can be displayed.

a) Refer to the 'Checklist for success' on the previous page when planning how to give your presentation, as you will be assessed by your peers and the teacher on these points.

b) You will also be reviewing other groups' work, then providing feedback, so make notes for each group's presentation against the criteria in the checklist, to enable you to do this.

c) Your group will receive feedback, too. After this happens, discuss the points as a group and explore:

- how effective your campaign was
- how well the team members contributed useful ideas
- how well everyone in the team was encouraged to participate
- how well conflict was resolved
- ways in which you could have worked together as a team more successfully.

❓ REFLECTION POINT

What is the role of teamwork in controlling the spread of disease? Consider these two points of view:

> Fighting disease is a team activity – societies control the spread of infection by shared actions.

> Fighting disease is about individual responsibility – keeping free from disease is about how you behave, nobody else.

- Suggest what might influence people to be more towards one viewpoint or the other.
- How could you carry out research into these different perspectives and what influences them?

Applying what you have learned

Skills focus
- ✓ Research
- ✓ Analysis
- ✓ Collaboration

Learning focus
- Research information relevant to questions raised and reference sources.
- Analyse information, identifying patterns and using evidence to support conclusions.
- Work effectively with people, developing ideas collaboratively to achieve an outcome.

Your task

Throughout history there have been outbreaks of infectious diseases. Sometimes these have died out relatively quickly and at other times they have reached **pandemic** proportions. Evidence suggests that those living in poverty are most affected. Each time there is a pandemic, the hope is expressed that we can be more ready for the next one.

Your task in this activity is to predict developments over the next 10 years that might make a pandemic more likely and more serious or that might help to stop diseases from spreading as quickly. There are several things to consider that may influence what you think, write and show. For example, you might give some thought to trends in:

- literacy rates and the role of education

- poverty, homelessness and **infant mortality**

- population growth and changes in the age profile – will there be more younger people in your country or is the proportion of older people increasing?

You need to make 3–5 key predictions, drawing on not only the work you have done in this chapter but also knowledge of global factors from Stages 7 and 8. These might include:

- climate change

- digitisation

- globalisation

- migration

- wealth inequality.

Your predictions will need to be supported by data and other evidence. You will need to collaborate as a team to research various ideas; this will involve you working together to select appropriate evidence and consider the quality of sources you plan to make use of. You will then need to agree on the analysis of the data and make a clear presentation of the findings.

Approaching the task

Refer to the 'Checklist for success' to support you as you plan how to approach the task. Then read through the two sample answers and teacher comments and consider the strengths and weaknesses of the students' writing. Further guidance on completing the task is given on page 21.

Vocabulary

pandemic: infectious disease that has spread across multiple continents

infant mortality: the number of deaths of children under the age of one for every thousand live births

Checklist for success

✔ Clearly developed and stated predictions. It should be clear what you think is likely to happen over the next 10 years and whether this is likely to make the spread of infectious diseases more or less likely in the future.

✔ A focus on the key question in this chapter as to how health is related to wealth.

✔ Good use of evidence to support predictions. Any claims you make need to be substantiated and, preferably, by reputable sources.

✔ Application of ideas and experiences from variety of sources. You should be able to draw on a wider understanding of infectious diseases and global trends.

✔ Recognition of both positive and negative aspects of the development as well as making an overall conclusion.

✔ Effective collaboration as a group to produce quality work.

Sample answer A writes about predicted growth in the use of virtual doctors.

Sample answer A:

We predict that the increasing use of virtual doctors over the next 10 years will tend to reduce the potential of infectious diseases to spread. By virtual doctors, we mean that either a patient can consult a doctor remotely using a tablet device and the internet, or the doctor could be a computer that is programmed to ask relevant questions, analyse the responses and prescribe a course of action.

Virtual medical consultations will mean that patients won't need to visit a medical facility that has many other sick and, in some cases, infectious people in it. It also means that consultations will be quicker and easier, so people will be more likely to consult a doctor and receive an expert opinion. This means that conditions will be caught at an earlier stage.

This is an interesting argument, which is clearly explained and well-reasoned, though it only explores arguments in favour. There is no data provided to support the view that this is a growing trend – there needs to be references to authoritative texts to support this viewpoint.

1 **a)** Sample answer A is clearly in favour of virtual doctors – suggest some of the arguments against this approach. For example, you might consider how accessible such provision would be to those living in poverty.

b) Are there any other points of feedback you would add to the teacher comment on sample answer A?

Sample answer B writes about the risk to humans from avian flu.

Sample answer B:

Our research shows that recent strains of avian flu present a risk to humans and that this risk is growing. We think it may well be that over the next 10 years the risk may increase and so humans will have to learn to protect themselves as well as reducing the impact on the bird population.

Several strains of avian flu can affect humans, and these have emerged relatively recently, suggesting that this may be a growing trend. It is reported by the WHO that the majority of cases 'have been associated with direct or indirect contact with infected live or dead poultry'; in other words, they have not been transmitted from human to human.

Education should be an important part of the forward strategy, both in terms of knowing the major risk factors but also understanding that it is not transmitted through routes such as eating eggs. The WHO suggests that 'Influenza viruses, with the vast silent reservoir in aquatic birds, are impossible to eradicate' but that the way forward is a combination of good personal protection for people in contact with birds, careful surveillance to spot outbreaks and the use of antiviral drugs in treatments.

This is a clearly expressed viewpoint with clear reasoning and supporting quotes of expert opinion. There is an effective indication suggesting a human response but less data to support the notion that this is likely to grow over the next 10 years.

2 **a)** Consider how the risk of contracting avian flu might correlate with poverty.

b) Are there any other points of feedback you would add to the teacher comment? For example, do you think this argument is balanced?

There are several steps you can take to succeed in producing a high-quality piece of work.

- Decide as a group on the issue or trend you are going to focus on. This might involve a bit of research to see what the potential issues are and then discussing and agreeing on a focus.

- Once you have a focus, decide as a group who is going to focus on what. For example, in the example above, different people could research the location and popularity of wildlife markets and the health risks of selling living or freshly killed wildlife.

- Gather the key points you have found and discuss what your overall response as a group is. You might find it useful to use a tool such as a PMI (Positive, Minus, Interesting) grid.

- Decide on an effective way of presenting your argument supported by your research findings.

- Get feedback on your work. Were others convinced by your prediction? Could you have made a stronger case?

- Listen to the other groups' predictions and consider how strong their arguments are. Which groups made a better case and why?

What is your teacher looking for?

- Clear demonstration that points from throughout the chapter and other parts of the course have been understood and applied.

- The capacity to identify key questions and draw on research findings to answer them, referencing sources appropriately.

- Ability to work effectively in a group, sharing ideas and allocating tasks.

Reflecting on your progress

Think back over the work you have done in this chapter:

- Describe what you feel is good practice when it comes to researching a topic or issue effectively.

- Give an example of where you feel you have done a good job of analysing the information gathered.

- Reflect on the effectiveness of the teams you worked in during this chapter in terms of achieving high quality outcomes.

Check your progress

Beginning	Developing	Going beyond
• I can construct a research question and follow it up.	• I can construct several relevant research questions and suggest which one to follow up.	• I can construct a range of relevant research questions and identify the most appropriate one to follow up.
• I can identify and reference a range of print and multimedia sources and use them to locate information.	• I can identify and reference a range of print and multimedia sources and use them to locate relevant information and answer research questions.	• I can identify and accurately reference a wide range of print and multimedia sources and use them to locate relevant information and answer research questions.
• I can select and record information from a range of sources and findings from primary research.	• I can select, organise and effectively record relevant information from a range of sources and findings from primary research, justifying the method chosen.	• I can select, organise and effectively record relevant information from a wide range of sources and findings from primary research, justifying the method chosen.
• I can identify a pattern or trend in graphical or numerical data.	• I can identify a pattern and trend in graphical or numerical data to support an argument or perspective.	• I can identify patterns and trends in graphical or numerical data in order to support an argument or perspective.
• I can work within a team to achieve a shared outcome and improve teamwork.	• I can work positively within a team to achieve a shared outcome and improve teamwork.	• I can collaborate positively and sensitively within a team to achieve a shared outcome and improve teamwork.

Next steps

Research another situation in which the spread of a disease could be limited if people understood more about the process of a disease and acted accordingly.

Review different health education information campaigns; consider how effective they are.

Research articles on global health trends in which data are used to support predictions; do you agree with the conclusions reached?

When working as a team, look to see who is taking a leadership role – how they are doing it and how well it is working.

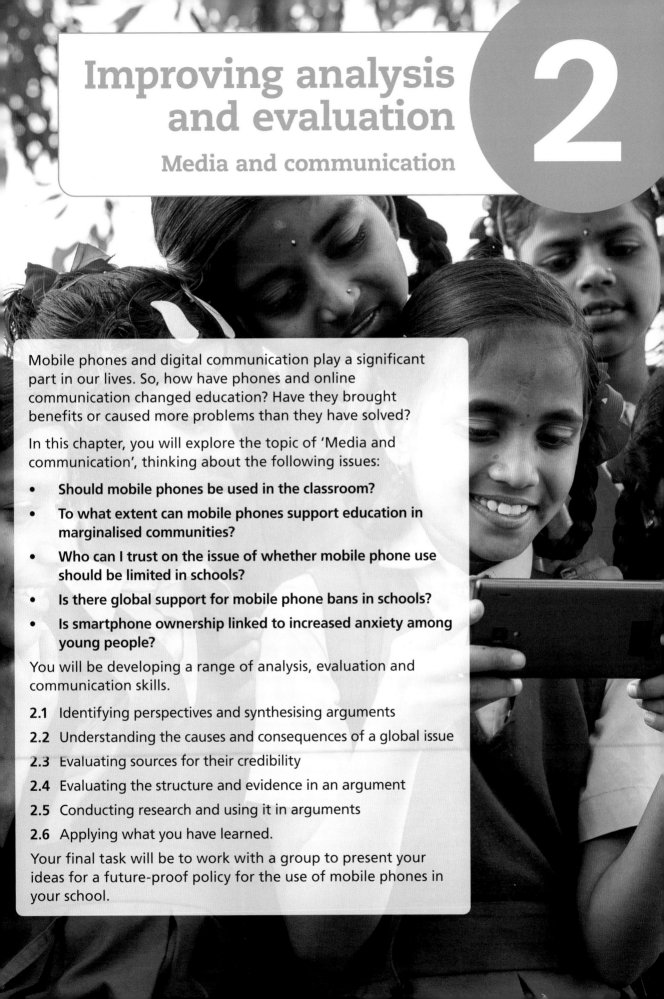

Improving analysis and evaluation

2

Media and communication

Mobile phones and digital communication play a significant part in our lives. So, how have phones and online communication changed education? Have they brought benefits or caused more problems than they have solved?

In this chapter, you will explore the topic of 'Media and communication', thinking about the following issues:

- **Should mobile phones be used in the classroom?**
- **To what extent can mobile phones support education in marginalised communities?**
- **Who can I trust on the issue of whether mobile phone use should be limited in schools?**
- **Is there global support for mobile phone bans in schools?**
- **Is smartphone ownership linked to increased anxiety among young people?**

You will be developing a range of analysis, evaluation and communication skills.

2.1 Identifying perspectives and synthesising arguments

2.2 Understanding the causes and consequences of a global issue

2.3 Evaluating sources for their credibility

2.4 Evaluating the structure and evidence in an argument

2.5 Conducting research and using it in arguments

2.6 Applying what you have learned.

Your final task will be to work with a group to present your ideas for a future-proof policy for the use of mobile phones in your school.

Identifying perspectives and synthesising arguments

Skills focus
✓ Analysis

Learning focus
- Identify perspectives from a range of sources.
- Synthesise arguments and evidence from a range of sources.

Big question: Should mobile phones be used in the classroom?

Getting started

In this chapter, you will think about what the best **policy** is for mobile phone use in schools. A good place to start is to think about your own experiences.

1 Discuss these questions with a partner:

   a) Are students allowed to use or bring mobile phones into the classroom in your school?

   b) Does your school have a policy on the use of phones in school? If so, what is it? Do students and teachers follow it?

Exploring

When exploring a **topical** issue such as this, there will be many different **perspectives**. Students will have their views, but so will parents, teachers, health organisations and governments – as will the multi-national companies that sell mobile phones or educational software. Making sense of these different perspectives and explaining them is an important skill.

A key perspective to establish first is your own.

2 What is your view on the use of mobile phones in school?

   a) Write down your opinion on the issue in a couple of simple sentences on a sticky note.

   b) Then add any reasons or arguments to support what you say. For example:

> I think mobile phones are important to have in school. The reason is that students can have their lesson timetable on it, so they are always prepared for class.

   c) Now, with your teacher's guidance, display your sticky note in the classroom.

Within your class, other students will have provided different perspectives to your own. When looking at different perspectives, it is important to consider the similarities and differences between them. Drawing together these similarities and differences and summing them up is called **synthesis**.

Synthesis is a very useful skill to have when trying to reach a general understanding of an issue without listing every individual view or piece of evidence.

3 Read through the display of sticky notes in your classroom.

Sum up those perspectives that are similar in a sentence or two. Then summarise any clear contrasting perspectives. You could start:

> *Many members of my class seem to think that…*
>
> *However, others feel that…*

> ### Key terms
>
> **perspective**: a viewpoint on an issue based on evidence and reasoning
>
> **synthesis**: combining ideas or points into a new text

Developing

Synthesising perspectives from longer written sources is a slightly more challenging skill. In this case, your first task is to make sure you understand what the individual perspectives are.

4 Read these two articles on the use of mobile phones in school. As you read, think about the overall view of each writer.

  a) Do the writers share the same viewpoint or do they disagree?

  b) What evidence or reasoning do they have for their view (if any)?

> ### Vocabulary
>
> **stance**: attitude towards something

The case for making classrooms phone-free

by Tyler Rablin, 6 June 2022

Two years ago, I was a champion for phones in the classroom. I was part of the team that was like, 'These are incredible! Let's bring them in and use them for learning!' I've recently changed my **stance**. Next year in my classroom, students will be checking in their phones when they arrive and getting them back on their way out the door. Why? Because attention is a limited resource and kids are spending too much of it distracted by their phones. It's a losing battle for kids and their brains.

When students pick up their phones, they are immediately **bombarded** with **notifications** and noise, and in my experience, this doesn't support learning. Are there creative tools and apps that are beneficial to learning? Yes, of course. But these tools and apps are not actively reaching out to them. Instead, it's **TikTok**, **Instagram** and games that are causing distraction. Their phones are actively and intentionally working against the goals of learning.

When we allow students to pick up their phones, even when we're using them for learning activities, it's too much temptation.

EdSurge, International Society for Technology in Education (ISTE).

How students can use mobiles to learn English

by Joanna Norton, 19 May 2014

I still use **desktops** in my class to access language-based websites and use Google Docs to allow students to work together. You can also connect a desktop computer to a whiteboard and project Google Images onto it. It's an invaluable resource for language teaching.

However, mobile devices allow you and your learners to interact **seamlessly** with each other, in both formal and informal learning contexts. For example, a teacher can encourage students to create a personal visual story about their daily routine. The student can take a series of **snapshots** of moments in their day — for example, their alarm clock, a toothbrush, a cup of coffee, their walk to work, etc. — and describe the actions to the teacher. For example, 'I take a shower and get dressed…' This will often highlight aspects of language that require teacher input.

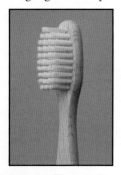

British Council.

Vocabulary

bombarded: continually sent huge amounts of information

notifications: alerts, such as pop-up text and images, often accompanied by sound

TikTok, Instagram: types of social media platform – applications in which users exchange information, images and videos

desktop: computer that sits on a desk or table and is not portable

seamlessly: smoothly; without interruption

snapshots: a series of photographs taken to provide a summary of an event

5 Working with a partner, discuss and write down answers to these questions:

a) What used to be Tyler Rablin's 'stance' on mobile phones?

b) How will Tyler's class next year be different? What reason do they give for their change in paragraph 1?

c) How does Tyler support this perspective with further evidence in paragraph 2?

d) What is their overall conclusion about phone use in the classroom?

e) Joanna Norton talks about another use of technology in the classroom – what is it, and how is it used?

f) What does she say is the main benefit of mobile devices for teachers and learners?

g) What example does she give to show how mobile phones support language learning?

6 Join up with another pair and, as a group, agree a simple summative paragraph that synthesises the two perspectives. You can use these prompts:

> On the one hand, Tyler Rablin believes that...
>
> This is because...
>
> However, Joanna Norton takes a different view and feels that...

Language support

When synthesising different perspectives, paraphrasing can help. This means using similar words or phrases to those used in the original source to show your understanding. For example, Tyler says phones are a 'distraction'. You could use synonyms such as 'interruption' or 'diversion', or explain they 'interfere' with learning.

Final task

7 Write a summary of 75–100 words of what you have learned or explored so far in this unit. Include:

- your initial thoughts about the use of mobile phones in school
- the policy (or lack of it) in your own school
- how your thoughts have developed, changed or stayed the same as a result of discussions and reading the two sources.

❓ REFLECTION POINT

This unit focuses largely on students in high school (from the age of 11 upwards). Should there be different mobile phone policies for students who are younger or older? Why?

You could research the mobile phone policies at your local primary school and nearest university.

Understanding the causes and consequences of a global issue

Skills focus

✓ Analysis

Learning focus

• Explain the causes of a global issue.

• Explain the consequences arising from a global issue.

Big question: To what extent can mobile phones support education in marginalised communities?

Getting started

Asif lives in a remote part of Pakistan. The nearest school is 20 miles away and there is no local bus to take him. When asked what single thing would improve his education, he said, 'Having a mobile phone'.

1　Discuss with a partner why you think Asif said this.

Exploring

The increased use of mobile phones, especially smartphones, has had several consequences. These include consequences for language and translation. For example, a refugee with a phone can use a translation app to convert what they say into the language of the country they are in.

2　Read the following extract from an article by an aid worker in Bangladesh, then note down answers to these questions:

a) What perspective about translation apps does the writer have? What evidence do they provide?

b) Is this a local/personal, national or global perspective on the issue? Why?

c) Could you use this source as part of an argument about the benefits (or otherwise) of using phones and digital devices for learning? Why/why not? What additional research might you need to do?

I worked in Bangladesh a decade ago and took lessons to learn Bengali. I learned some of the grammar rules and some basic vocabulary. When I returned this year, I could still remember some of this, but I found that I constantly used a voice translation app when speaking to refugees. It meant I could communicate a much wider variety of ideas. Did it help my own learning? Hmm. I'm not sure. I couldn't remember many of the phrases, whereas the 'old' ones I learned 'properly' stuck in my head.

In trying to widen your research into how mobile phones and digital learning generally can improve lives, you identify the following article from Children on the Edge, a charity that supports children and promotes their rights.

Delivering education to refugee children through digital

contributed by Children on the Edge, 2 March 2021

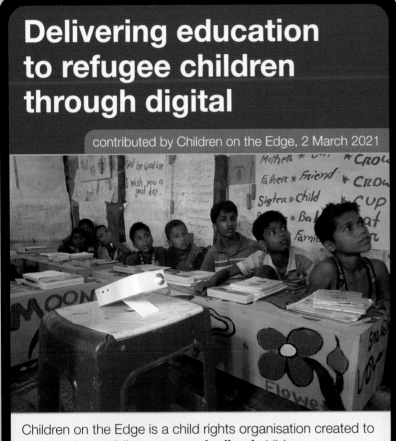

Children on the Edge is a child rights organisation created to support the world's most **marginalised** children.

They currently work with more than 20 000 children in Bangladesh, India, Uganda, Myanmar and Lebanon. Over thirty years of experience in more than 18 countries have enabled them to work alongside communities to design programmes that address their specific needs and circumstances.

This **recipe** focuses on the charity's work delivering education to the **Rohingya** children in the refugee camps of Bangladesh.

Whilst authorities in Bangladesh permit education for Rohingya refugees, there are strict rules around teaching the children only in the Burmese and English languages – not in the local Bengali language or in the dialect the Rohingya speak, which has no universally accepted script.

Vocabulary

marginalised: being ignored or treated as though you are insignificant

recipe: set of instructions

Rohingya: ethnic group from Rakhine state, Myanmar (formerly Burma)

The COVID-19 pandemic further accelerated the need for digital learning, because charity staff members could not be brought in and teachers within the camps could not leave to undergo training.

Alongside face-to-face teaching, learning is now delivered digitally every day. The curriculum is transformed into colourful, fun visual video lessons where much material is translated or **dubbed**. 75 teachers are given smartphones and sent lessons via USB memory sticks, which they project onto a screen via battery-powered projectors. These visual and verbal video lessons break down the language barrier and enable genuine understanding and meaningful learning.

Vocabulary

dubbed: replaced by a voice recording in the audience's language

Catalyst website.

One of the many consequences of being a refugee is that you may be forced to leave your own country and travel somewhere where a different language is spoken.

3 Working on your own, make notes on the extent to which national *and* global issues are addressed in this article.

a) What is the *main* issue that Children on the Edge as an organisation addresses (as stated in the first two sentences)? Is it a local, national or global issue?

b) How does the article shift focus to a specific place and people? Is this local, national or global?

4 Now, think about the causes and consequences. Write answers to the following questions:

a) What was the main cause for teachers needing to use digital learning?

b) What was one consequence of lockdown on where children were educated?

c) What consequences were there in terms of how children learned?

5 Considering all you have read, write a sentence or two explaining the overall perspective of the writer on the use of mobile phones and online platforms for refugees. What specific words or phrases in the final paragraph suggest this?

This response to the article tries to summarise the writer's perspective. It receives this feedback:

> A consequence of being a refugee is being ignored by governments and media, and is a global issue. These refugees suffered because of their language. Covid-19 didn't help because teachers couldn't be trained or leave the camps. However, using online platforms to teach has helped.

This is a good answer because it highlights the global nature of the perspective. However, when it moves on to the 'refugees', it is imprecise and could provide more detail. It touches on one of the causes and consequences of the issue but misses others out. It would help to reference the article directly.

6 **a)** How is the following response better? Discuss with a partner.

> According to the article 'Delivering education to refugee children through digital', a consequence of being a refugee is being ignored by governments and media. This is a global issue, but the article focuses on a national one – the plight of Rohingya refugees in Bangladesh. They suffer because…

b) Working on your own, complete this response by:

- explaining the consequences of the children being Bangladeshi speakers

- explaining how digital learning helped (both students and teachers)

- summing up the overall perspective of the writer. Include at least one quotation from the text to support what you say.

Final task

7 Revisit the big question for this unit: 'To what extent can mobile phones support education in marginalised communities?'

Write a response of 125–150 words in which you give your perspective on whether mobile phone and digital communication has improved people's lives. You can use these prompts if you wish.

> One consequence of the availability of mobile phones is…
>
> This has helped/hindered people by…
>
> An example of this is…
>
> This gives a local/national/global perspective because…

❓ REFLECTION POINT

Think about a national or global issue you care strongly about. Note down what you believe the main causes and consequences of it are.

When you have finished, look at what you have written – are you able to identify the causes and consequences in your explanation? How are they different?

Evaluating sources for their credibility

Skills focus
✓ Evaluation
Learning focus
- Read and understand a range of sources and supporting sources.
- Learn to judge how credible different sources are.

Big question: Who can I trust on the issue of whether mobile phone use should be limited in schools?

Getting started

1   Imagine your friend is playing music loudly through their headphones. You are worried it's damaging their hearing. How would you approach persuading them that it's not a good idea? Would telling them yourself be enough?

Discuss this issue briefly with a partner and decide how you would tackle it.

Exploring

When you seek advice or information, being able to trust or believe what you read or hear is very important. There are several key factors to bear in mind, as shown in the table.

The source itself	• Is it **valid**? For example, when was it written or produced; is it out of date? • Is it relevant? For example, does it meet your research needs?
The author/ organisation who wrote or produced it	• Who are they? Do they have any **expertise** in this area? • Do they have a **vested interest**? Are they **biased**?
Purpose of author/ organisation	• Are they trying to inform you, persuade you, shock you into action – or something else? (This links to 'vested interest'.) • How do they gain, if at all, from what they write or say?
Evidence or support for what they say	• How **credible** is their argument? • Does the author refer to any other sources to support their perspective? If so, are those sources credible?

2 Think again about question 1. Discuss this question with a partner:

Would an article about noise damage by an **audiologist** that mentions a report from a top hospital on hearing loss represent a credible source? Why/why not?

Now, imagine you have been given the job of deciding your school's policy on the use of mobile phones by students. As a result of your work in this chapter so far and your own reflections, you probably have a perspective on this. However, if you simply assert your view, without evidence, then it is not very useful guidance. You need to explore trusted sources.

3 During their research, a student identified the sources shown in the table below (one of which you saw in Unit 2.1) and made some basic notes about each one. Based solely on these initial notes, which ones do you think are credible? Make your own brief notes on each, explaining your thinking. For example:

> Article 'Banning mobile phones in schools….' – author is a professor of economics in an educational institution, so has some expertise...

Source title	Author/organisation	Date and location	Notes
'Banning mobile phones in schools can improve students' academic performance. This is how we know'	Louis-Philippe Beland, Assistant Professor of Economics, Carleton University, Canada	21 March 2021 www.theconversation.com	Argues for banning phones in schools based on studies done
'Mobile learning during Covid-19: One-to-one instruction through phone calls can be effective when schooling is disrupted'	Noam Angrist, columnist Researcher at the University of Oxford	24 July 2022 www.katmandupost.com	Refers to studies in Botswana on the benefits of mobile phones in learning
'10 advantages to allowing kids to have cell phones in schools'	'Guest blogger' (writer not named)	2011 www.parentingskillsblog.com	Lists advantages – mostly for parents
'The case for making classrooms phone-free'	Tyler Rablin, English teacher	6 June 2022 www.edsurge.com	Explains why changed their mind on phones in school based on own experience and secondary research

A key element in judging how valid or credible a source is, is whether you can find other sources that support its perspective.

4 From the students' list of sources in the table on the previous page, which (if any) seem to support the 'Banning mobile phones in schools…' article? Write a sentence or two in response, explaining why.

Developing

A further element in judging a source's credibility is deciding whether the source – or author – is biased. You can often judge that something is biased when it:

- relies solely or mainly on personal experience or evidence

- uses generalised or sweeping statements about groups of people or organisations

- asserts views without any real supporting evidence

- refers to evidence that is selective or simplistic, ignoring other **counterevidence**.

5 Read the following opening to a blog by a technology reporter. In what way is the blog biased? Make some notes, referring to the list of factors above when making a judgement.

Technology News

BLOG HOME   ABOUT ME   LINKS   ARCHIVE

IT'S THE TEACHERS' FAULT

It's no surprise teachers are against mobile phones being used in schools. After all, all teachers want to do is make learning boring and predictable. They hate anything modern. They want to stick to the old ways and ignore all the benefits of using phones to help learning. Take my old English teacher: they hated anything new and wouldn't even use whiteboards, preferring the old-fashioned chalkboard.

The bias in the technology reporter's blog is obvious and extreme. However, bias can often be more difficult to detect when it is presented in reasonable language. Here, a school principal writes to parents about a new policy.

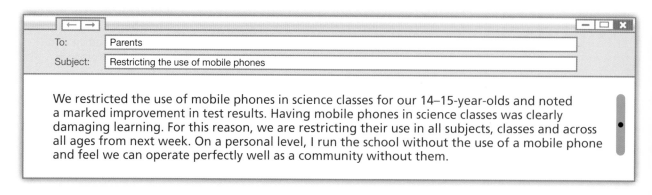

To: Parents

Subject: Restricting the use of mobile phones

We restricted the use of mobile phones in science classes for our 14–15-year-olds and noted a marked improvement in test results. Having mobile phones in science classes was clearly damaging learning. For this reason, we are restricting their use in all subjects, classes and across all ages from next week. On a personal level, I run the school without the use of a mobile phone and feel we can operate perfectly well as a community without them.

6 **a)** In what way is the principal's rationale **flawed**? Think about the steps the writer makes from one statement or belief to another.

b) In what other ways might this statement be biased?

Final task

7 Read one of the articles listed in the table or identify a new source on the issue of mobile phone use in schools. Read it carefully and then make a judgement on how credible it is. Use the 'Checklist for success' to help you.

Checklist for success

✔ Evaluate the validity of the source – is it up to date and relevant? Does it come from a credible publication/organisation?

✔ Find out as much as you can about the author, their background and area/level of expertise. Do they have a vested interest? Is their perspective biased?

✔ Evaluate the evidence in the source and the argument made. How flawed or logical is it? Have supporting sources been cited or evidence used?

---

8 Swap your source and comments with a partner.

a) Decide whether you agree with your partner's source evaluation. Change or add to it as needed.

b) When you get your own source evaluation back, consider your partner's evaluation – did they agree or disagree with you?

🔑 Key terms

counterevidence: facts or information that supports an alternative viewpoint

flawed: based on a false logic

❓ REFLECTION POINT

In more general terms, the date when a source was produced or when evidence was quoted is also important in evaluating a source. If the writer of an article about phone use refers to a '2015 paper', does this date matter? How might it affect what you think about phone usage in schools?

Evaluating the structure and evidence in an argument

Skills focus
✓ Evaluation
Learning focus
• Identify the structure, reasoning and evidence in an argument.
• Evaluate the argument's strength in relation to these factors.

Big question: Is there global support for mobile phone bans in schools?

Getting started

1. What do you know about other schools and education systems around the world? Can you think of any reasons why particular countries – or regions – might be more likely to ban or encourage the use of phones in education?

   a) Discuss these questions with a partner and then share your ideas with another pair.

   b) What did you agree or disagree about?

Exploring

Once you have made a judgement about whether a source is credible, you need to evaluate the argument itself. There are several things to look for in a well-argued text:

• a clear introduction that sets out what the issue is/makes you realise its importance

• the use of relevant evidence

• a wide range of evidence (where appropriate)

• conclusions drawn from the evidence that are logical, reasonable and rational.

2. Bearing these factors in mind, read this extract from the 'Banning mobile phones in schools...' article.

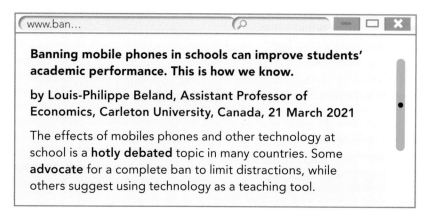

www.ban...

Banning mobile phones in schools can improve students' academic performance. This is how we know.

by Louis-Philippe Beland, Assistant Professor of Economics, Carleton University, Canada, 21 March 2021

The effects of mobiles phones and other technology at school is a **hotly debated** topic in many countries. Some **advocate** for a complete ban to limit distractions, while others suggest using technology as a teaching tool.

> **Vocabulary**
>
> **hotly debated**: strongly argued
>
> **advocate**: speak up for

Kids in public South Australian primary schools started the school year without being allowed to bring their mobile phones to class, unless they are needed for class activity. All students in public Western Australian, Victorian, and Tasmanian schools have a mobile phone ban in place… for all or some of 2020. New South Wales also banned mobile phones in public primary schools, with secondary schools having the option to opt in, since the start of 2020. Education departments have introduced the bans for various reasons including to improve academic outcomes and decrease bullying.

Several recent papers point to [the] positive impact[s] of banning mobile phones at school on student performance and other outcomes. Understanding the evidence is crucial for best policy. In a 2015 paper, we used a method – called a difference-in-difference strategy – as well as student data from England to investigate the effect of banning mobile phones on student performance. In this method, we compared schools that have had phones removed to similar schools with no phone bans. This allowed us to isolate the effect of mobiles phones on student performance from other factors that could affect performance.

We found banning mobile phones at school leads to an increase in student performance. Our results suggest that after schools banned mobile phones, test scores of students aged 16 increased by 6.4% of a **standard deviation**. This is equivalent to adding five days to the school year or an additional hour a week. The effects were twice as large for low-achieving students, and we found no impact on high-achieving students. Our results suggest low-performing students are more likely to be distracted by the presence of mobile phones, while high-performing students can focus with or without mobile phones.

The results of our paper suggest banning mobile phones has considerable benefits including a reduction in the gap between high- and low-achieving students. This is substantial improvement for a low-cost education policy.

Recent studies from Spain and Norway, using a similar **empirical** strategy to ours, also show **compelling** evidence on the benefit of banning mobile phones on student performance, with similar effect size. In Spain, banning mobile phones has been shown to increase students' scores in maths and science. Researchers also **documented** a decrease in incidences of bullying.

The Conversation.

🔑 Key terms

standard deviation: a measure of how dispersed the data is in relation to the mean average

empirical: based on observation or experience

Vocabulary

compelling: persuasive; creating strong interest or admiration

documented: recorded, written down

3 Write brief answers to these questions related to the article's argument.

a) How does the opening paragraph introduce the topic? Is it clear what the subject will be?

b) What examples does the writer refer to in the second paragraph? Can this be viewed as supporting evidence of the writer's perspective? Why/why not?

c) In what way is the evidence presented in paragraphs 3 and 4 relevant?

d) What conclusions were drawn from this evidence in paragraphs 4 and 5? Are these conclusions logical? For example, the writer claims in paragraph 3 that 'other factors' which might have affected performance were 'isolated.' How does this help the claim/conclusion in paragraph 4?

e) How does the final paragraph further support the argument? What evidence is given – and how is it different from what has been explained previously?

US President Barack Obama speaks at the Lincoln Memorial on 28 August 2013.

Developing

It is important to recognise the way skilled writers and speakers use language to make their arguments and evidence more persuasive. Famous speakers such as Barack Obama and Greta Thunberg use both evidence *and* powerful emotion to get their points across.

Understanding this can help you understand both the argument and the way in which the writer wishes to influence you. Look for language related to:

Climate and environmental activist Greta Thunberg

	Language that may be used
…focusing in on evidence and describing its effects	'This suggests/indicates/shows/reveals/points to…', 'We found/discovered that…', 'According to a survey…'
…identifying trends or patterns	'more/less likely', 'greater/fewer', 'increase/decrease in…'
…the strength or emotional power of the writer's vocabulary	'clear that…', 'compelling/indisputable evidence that…', 'we know…'

However, take care to separate the language used from the content of the evidence. You need to be objective in judging the argument on its merits, not its persuasive force.

4 Working with a partner, find and note down examples of the following in the 'Banning mobile phones in school' article:

   a) focusing in on evidence and describing effects

   b) identifying trends or patterns

   c) emotive language.

Final task

5 Write a 100–125-word summary of the 'Banning mobile phones in school' article, focusing on the argument and how strong or weak it is. Comment on:

   • the content (in terms of evidence and language)

   • the structure (clarity and logic).

6 These are two extracts from responses to the article. How is Response B better?

Response A:

The argument is effective because it starts by clearly introducing the issue. The second paragraph provides evidence of research in regions of Australia where phones have been banned. This clearly links with the opening introduction. It is relevant and valid as it is from 2020 and refers to lots of different regions.

True – this makes the argument easier to follow.

This is evidence, but the writer does not draw any conclusions from it.

True, but unless the writer reveals the results of the policy, the evidence is meaningless.

Response B:

The writer begins by setting out the issue clearly. The second paragraph provides a national perspective on the issue that is relevant and valid, but by simply stating the research took place and not revealing its results on learning, it undermines the credibility of the argument in general. When the writer does quote further research and its results, it is from 2015. This is a problem because…

❓ REFLECTION POINT

Based on the article, is it true to say there is global support for banning mobile phones? Why/why not?

Discuss this question with a partner. What further research might be needed to find out?

Conducting research and using it in arguments

Skills focus
✓ Research
Learning focus
- Choose a research method that meets your needs for the final task in the chapter.
- Test your predictions using the methods you have chosen.

Big question: Is smartphone ownership linked to increased anxiety among young people?

Getting started

1   In pairs, discuss the terms 'primary research' and 'secondary research'. Recall any examples of research you have done, and what type it was.

Exploring

When you use data from research to support an argument, it is likely to demonstrate trends and patterns.

A trend is an upwards or downwards shift (move) in a data set over time. For example:

> A study in the UK revealed that in 2012, 19% of 55–64-year-olds owned smartphones. In 2019, it was 55% and by 2021, it was 83%.

A trend can be part of a pattern. Patterns also include the way data is grouped or **clustered** together, what **spread** they show, and so on. For example:

> A survey of national mobile phone use showed tight clusters of smartphone ownership in city centres. Smartphone ownership in less-industrialised areas was more spread out.

You will also need to be aware of whether the data provides a local, national or global perspective.

2 Look at this set of graphical data.

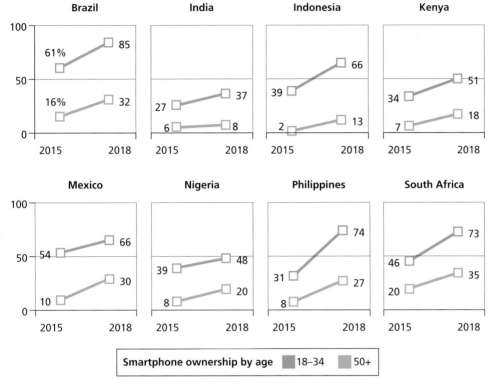

In many emerging economies, younger people lead the way in smartphone ownership.

Smartphone ownership by age ■ 18–34 ■ 50+

Note: Data for people aged 35–49 years not shown.
Percentage of adults that own a smartphone in selected emerging countries.
Pew Research Center/Spring 2018 Global Attitudes Survey.

a) Does this data set give you a local, national or global perspective?

b) How would you describe the trend in smartphone ownership among 18–34-year-olds between 2015 and 2018 in Indonesia and the Philippines?

c) Every country but one shows over 10% growth in smartphone ownership in the 50+ category. Which country 'bucks' (goes against) this trend?

d) Can you identify any overall global trends? (Is the headline above the data set correct?)

c) How useful is this data set for exploring current trends in smartphone ownership?

So how could you use this sort of research in your own work? You need to decide:

* what you wish to find out (this might involve predicting a trend or pattern)

* what research method you will use

* how you will make sense of the data you generate.

Imagine a student called Amy wants to find out if owning a smartphone increases or decreases levels of anxiety among young people aged 7–18 years. She thinks that finding a trend over time might be difficult as it's not possible to interview people in the past. However, she can look at patterns through clusters or spreads. For example, she predicts that anxiety will be greater among older students.

Amy asks several students in her school this question: 'On a scale of 1–10 (with 1 being 'not at all' and 10 being 'very strongly'), how much does spending time on a phone in school make you feel anxious?'

She records the **mean average** results in the table below.

7–9 years	10–12 years	13–15 years	16–18 years
3	5	8	6

3 Make notes in answer to the following questions:

a) Did the data Amy gathered match her prediction?

b) Which age group of students had the highest levels of anxiety?

c) If Amy conducted the same survey with students in a year's time, what trends might she be able to identify?

d) What other factors may have influenced these results?

Developing

In terms of supporting an argument, data such as Amy's could be useful in offering guidance on mobile phone use in schools. However, she would need to be careful not to confuse **correlation** with **causation**. For example, the sharp rise in ownership of phones among Brazilians may correlate with a reduction in the cost of phones. However, this does not prove causation. Other factors might have been more influential – for example, the extension of phone network coverage.

Have a look at this extract from a sample report based on Amy's research.

> My own analysis suggests that anxiety around phone use is highest between ages 13 and 15. Therefore, it might be sensible to limit phone use in school for students in these grades, and perhaps offer some sort of counselling support aimed specifically at this age group.

4 Discuss with a friend whether this suggestion is reasonable given the research findings. Consider:

a) Does she need more information before proposing this solution?

b) Is she right to focus solely on this age group? Why?

Key terms

mean average: the total of all scores divided between the number of scores. For example, if six students give scores of 5, 6, 6, 8, 6, 5, the mean average is 36 ÷ 6, which is 6.

correlation: relationship between two sets of data

causation: the cause of a change

For the final task in this chapter, you will be recommending what your school's mobile phone policy should be. To support your arguments, you can draw on secondary sources you have read, but you will also need to carry out primary research.

The primary research methods you could use include:

- interviews, supported by a set of questions that you plan beforehand

- surveys – questionnaires using **open** and **closed questions** to find out specific information; these could include **multiple choice** responses

- observations – for example, watching how a group of students behaves

- focus groups – selected groups of people with whom you can 'test' out ideas or share questions on a specific focus – for example, opinions on a new mathematics app for studying.

5 What are the strengths and limitations of each of these primary research methods? Working with a partner, create a table listing the advantages and disadvantages for each.

Key terms

open questions: questions that generate a range of answers with no defined length. For example: 'How do you feel if you have to spend time without your phone?'

closed questions: questions with a limited or set range of responses. For example: 'Do you own a mobile phone?'

multiple choice: questions that provide a set number of given responses to choose from. For example: 'How do you use your phone for educational purposes? A: internet for homework, B: revision apps, C: calculator, D: other

Final task

6 In a small group, discuss between you what primary research you will do, the methods you will use, and what you hope to find out. Record your plans in a table like the one below.

Student name	Aim of research	Research method	Timescale
Amy	Find out levels of anxiety caused by phone use	Questionnaire	Distribute week beginning 7 May. Collect 14 May.

7 Carry out the primary research you have planned in your group and then report back. Work together to:

- draw out any findings from the research

- identify any flaws in it

- follow up any further research that needs to be done.

8 Finally, in your groups, return to the 'big question' for this unit and discuss: 'Is smartphone ownership linked to increased anxiety among young people?' How well is your group now able to answer this question?

? REFLECTION POINT

What would be the most effective way to present your research findings? For example, you might consider slide displays, visual representations such as pie charts, spoken explanations supported with images. Make notes to explain your thinking.

Applying what you have learned

Skills focus
- ✓ Analysis
- ✓ Evaluation
- ✓ Communication

Learning focus
- Analyse and evaluate arguments and evidence around a key issue.
- Present a well-reasoned and clearly structured solution to your peers that draws on research findings.

Your task

You will work as part of a group to present your ideas for a **future-proof** policy for the use of mobile phones in your school. This will be a presentation lasting no more than 15 minutes.

Approaching the task

Each member of the group will contribute to each stage as set out below.

1. Reviewing your work so far

Begin by reviewing the research and evidence you have already looked at in this chapter and any you have conducted yourself. In your group, draw together your findings and any conclusions you have reached jointly about the positive or negative aspects of mobile phone use in schools. You will need to consider:

- local perspectives (your own school/area)

- national perspectives (your country or region)

- global perspectives (multiple regions or the world as a whole).

Keep a group record of your decisions. This will help shape your final presentation to your teacher and class.

> Based on our research so far, we believe that…
>
> This is supported by local research in the form of…
>
> In addition, we looked at national perspectives through…
>
> And the global view in the form of…

2. Identifying the need for further research and carrying it out

Now, consider whether you need to find out more on the issue. Do you have sufficient data? Have you considered arguments on both sides of the issue? Have you found out enough about how schools globally approach mobile phone use?

Once you have decided, follow up by researching and analysing further sources. Add notes to your record.

> After reviewing our research, we concluded we needed to know more about…
>
> So, we identified the following additional sources…

3. Evaluating sources

Now, write a brief evaluation of the key sources you intend to use.

> We evaluated the core sources we looked at and decided that the most credible were…
>
> This was because…
>
> A compelling/logical/reasonable argument was made by…
>
> This was because the writer…

4. Synthesising what you have learned

Now, bring together all aspects of your research and evidence. Write a summative note, synthesising the different perspectives you have identified and drawing an overall conclusion.

> Overall, the arguments for the use of mobile phones in schools can be summarised as…
>
> The counterarguments are…

5. Shaping your own ideas

This is the central element of your task. You must now decide what your recommendations about mobile phone use policy in your schools should be. You might wish to consider:

- a general ban or complete freedom of use
- a restriction or limit (for example, for different ages, subjects, contexts, times of day)
- teacher recommendations to increase or decrease use (for example, to use educational apps more or less)
- restrictions or increased connections to school intranet or external internet
- guidance or education for students, teachers and parents on responsible usage
- innovative ways of using phones (if use is not banned)
- sanctions or rewards for misuse or positive use
- how the policy might need to change as phones evolve further (for example, due to wearable technology)
- how you will ensure the policy takes account of national and global perspectives.

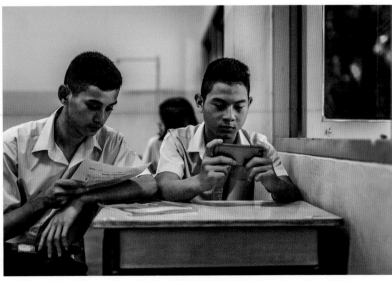

Discuss your ideas as a group carefully and then decide on a five-point 'mission statement' about mobile phone use in schools.

> OUR MISSION STATEMENT ABOUT MOBILE PHONE USE IN SCHOOL
>
> Our school will ensure that:
>
> 1. No student will be disadvantaged if they do not own a mobile phone
>
> 2. There will be a limit on usage by…

6. Supporting your policy

For each of the five points in your mission statement, you will need to support your views with evidence you have gathered. For example:

> It is important students are not disadvantaged if they do not have mobile phones. As 'The Times of India' reported in its article about Covid, 'When education goes all digital, students without smartphones fall behind' (9 April 2020); students in more well-off schools can be supported but those in poorer areas are less fortunate.
>
> Another aspect to consider is the anxiety of not having a phone to hand. In our in-school surveys, we found that 65 per cent of students felt isolated when they couldn't text or communicate with friends easily…

7. Finishing off

As this is a spoken presentation, you will need to conclude with a 'call to action' – a final few words drawing together your group's overall perspective and hopes for the future.

> We believe that by following this guidance, our school will ensure that…
>
> Therefore, the next steps must be to…

8. Preparing for the presentation

The preparatory work above should have provided the basic outline for your presentation, but you will need to agree as a group a few things before you rehearse and then deliver your presentation.

- Who will speak – and in what order?

- Will there be any visual support for your presentation, such as a slide display? If so, you will need to allow additional time to prepare this.

- How will you make your presentation engaging and interesting? (Will you use a mobile phone as part of your presentation, for example?)

- Will you have a question and answer session? If so, who will respond to any queries about your plans?

Use the 'Checklist for success' to help with finalising your presentation content.

Checklist for success

✔ Explain clearly what you were trying to achieve.

✔ Distinguish between any local, national and global research.

✔ Use the relevant terms to explain data such as 'trends' and 'patterns'.

✔ Use your primary research findings and other secondary sources to support the argument you present.

✔ Make clear where you are highlighting causes and consequences.

✔ Where necessary, highlight any flaws or limitations in what you have found out or propose.

---

9. Delivering the presentation

Now, give your presentation, lasting no more than 15 minutes, to the class and your teacher. Use the 'Checklist for success' to help you deliver a spoken presentation.

Checklist for success

✔ Speak clearly and look positive/smile.

✔ Look at your audience.

✔ Use hand gestures to illustrate points.

✔ Change the pitch and tone of your voice to make it sound interesting.

✔ Avoid interrupting other members of your group.

✔ Use clear, sequencing language to show how your presentation is linked coherently – for example, 'As Asif just said…', 'Now, we are going to look at…', 'A further aspect to be considered is…', 'To conclude…'

Reflecting on your progress

Think back over your group's presentation. How effectively did you communicate your ideas?

If someone was applying the same criteria you explored for analysis and evaluation of arguments to your presentation, how do you think they would have scored you on a scale of 1 (low) to 10 (high)? Why?

In what ways was your argument effective? Where could it be improved?

Check your progress

Beginning

- I can identify the overall perspective in more than one source.

- I understand what causes and consequences are when looking at issues.

- I understand the factors for evaluating a source's credibility.

- I can identify the core elements of a well-structured argument.

- I can understand and use some different research methods.

- I can help plan and participate in a presentation of a group proposal.

Developing

- I can draw together the different arguments from sources and explain them clearly.

- I can explain how a writer uses causes and consequences to make a point.

- I can evaluate a source in a range of ways, including its credibility and validity.

- I can explain how an argument is structured in terms of its logic, evidence and conclusions.

- I can make predictions for research and test them using a range of research methods.

- I can explain a proposal to solve an issue and present it effectively.

Going beyond

- I can synthesise both the arguments and the evidence from a range of sources.

- I can explain local, national and global causes and consequences.

- I can evaluate a range of sources and supporting sources for their credibility and validity.

- I can evaluate the strength of an argument based on a wide range of factors.

- I can evaluate data and trends from local, national and global research.

- I can communicate research findings and present them as part of a proposal.

Next steps

Create a poster with three circles increasing in size from the middle. Within the circles, record perspectives about mobile phone use in education at a local (inner circle), national (middle circle) and global (outer circle) level.

Find out about the most up-to-date language translation apps, how they work and how effective they are for everyday and academic use. Create a 'Top five' chart, listing the features, advantages and disadvantages of each.

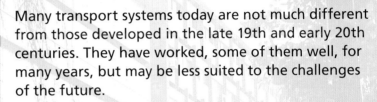

Solving problems, suggesting outcomes

Transport, travel and tourism

3

Many transport systems today are not much different from those developed in the late 19th and early 20th centuries. They have worked, some of them well, for many years, but may be less suited to the challenges of the future.

In this chapter, you will explore the topic of 'Transport, travel and tourism', thinking about the following issues:

- **What is a good way of getting around in the 21st century?**

- **How can we design the best transport system for a location?**

- **What problems does transport have to solve as well as moving people around?**

- **What is the best way of using a team to make an impression?**

- **When is it OK for an expert to change their mind?**

You will be developing a range of collaboration, communication, analysis and reflection skills.

3.1 Working as a team to achieve a shared goal

3.2 Discussing information and developing understanding

3.3 Recommending action to address an issue

3.4 Reflecting on how a team can improve and succeed

3.5 Explaining how exploring different perspectives changes minds

3.6 Applying what you have learned.

Your final task will be to use ideas you have developed over the chapter to suggest the most effective solution to a transport system that satisfies a range of requirements.

Working as a team to achieve a shared goal

Skills focus
✓ Collaboration
Learning focus
• Work flexibly and cooperatively as a team to achieve an outcome.
• Undertake specialist roles within a team.

Big question: What is a good way of getting around in the 21st century?

Getting started

Imagine you and a group of friends arrive in a new holiday destination. You want to explore it for a few days. Here are three of the local travel options:

There are tuk-tuks for hire. You could use these to be driven to places you want to visit.

You could each buy a visitor's bus pass. This will provide you with access to the local services.

You could buy a map and explore on foot.

1 Working in a small group, discuss your responses to these questions:

   a) For each travel option, identify the advantages and disadvantages.

   b) Decide which one you would probably use and explain why.

   c) Suggest why someone who is a resident in the town might make a different decision to your group.

2 Now review your group working skills during the 'Getting started' task using the 'Checklist for success'. How well did you manage the sharing of ideas and decision making; was everyone involved and happy with the outcome? How could you improve individually and as a team?

Checklist for success

✔ Share ideas with the rest of the group, explaining your reasoning.

✔ Listen carefully to others' contributions, asking questions about their ideas and suggesting ways of building on them.

✔ Be willing to compromise so that other people can be more involved.

✔ Be ready to change your view if someone offers a different point of view that is convincing.

✔ Be loyal to the team view – once you've agreed on an approach, all team members should represent this view.

Your group has been asked to make recommendations for an effective local transport system for residents and tourists. It needs to be cheap and reliable, but there are other considerations.

✔ It must work in all weathers
– whether it's raining, below freezing or very hot.

✔ It needs to work for those with limited mobility – for example, wheelchair users or those unable to manage steep steps.

✘ It shouldn't add to pollution – the air quality in some towns is quite poor and some types of transport cause a lot of pollution.

✔ It should be able to carry goods as well as people.

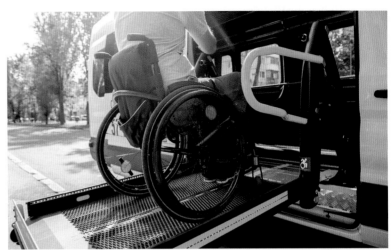

3 As a group, discuss the three types of transport from the 'Getting started' task – tuk-tuk, bus and walking – in the light of the above requirements.

a) How well would each type meet those concerns?

b) Are there other considerations that should be applied?

c) Which mode of transport is best considering your discussions? Why? Remember to:

- support your ideas with clear reasoning

- build on other people's suggestions.

Developing

In many organisations, people have specialist roles and are expected to work in teams. In this chapter, you will take on a specialist role. Remember, though, that even though you have a specialist perspective, you still need to collaborate effectively as a team.

The roles are:

- *Accountant:* this person will make sure the transport system covers its costs. There needs to be money coming in to pay for staff wages, repairs and maintenance of equipment, etc. If money spent is greater than monies earned, the service will close.

- *Environmental Protection Officer:* this person will work to limit the negative environmental impact of the transport system. This might include consideration of noise or air pollution, or damage to the landscape by construction work.

- *Inclusion Manager:* this person will make sure the transport system meets the needs of a wide a range of people, including children, the elderly, individuals with a disability and those who do not speak the local language.

- *Sales Manager:* this person is responsible for promoting the transport service. They will need to make the service appeal to all types of customers.

4 **a)** Working on your own, consider each of the roles. List the key skills you think would be important for someone taking on that role to have. They might, for example, need to be good with numbers or an effective communicator.

Make notes on what you anticipate will be the most difficult thing about each role. You could set these notes out as a table.

b) Compare notes with other students to see if you have come up with similar responses.

5 In your group, allocate the specialist roles. You will need to think about what kind of role each team member is best suited to. For example:

- You may prefer to allocate roles based on people's skills and prior experience, so team members are given a job they know they can do well.

- Alternatively, team members might want to take on a new role they have little experience in, as this will be an opportunity to develop new skills.

- It may be that you have several people interested in one role and no one volunteering for another. This might be the first thing you have to sort out as a group. You could do this by discussion or by voting, for example.

Once all the roles have been allocated, note down who is doing which role and why.

Final task

You are now going to review the three transport methods – tuk-tuk, bus and walking – in your specialist role.

6 Working on your own, make some notes about the advantages and disadvantages of each form of transport. For example, if you are an Environmental Protection Officer, you might consider how each form of transport affects the surrounding area – the noise it makes, the pollution it emits and how it impacts the landscape visually.

Decide which form of transport would be the best. You need to be prepared to justify your decision.

7 Now share your ideas and see what the group thinks overall about each form of transport. Use the language support box to aid your discussions.

8 What did you agree as a group about the best form of transport? Create a spider diagram, flow diagram or mind map to summarise:

a) how each group specialist inputted to the decision-making process

b) the decisions reached as a group with reasons why.

❓ REFLECTION POINT

What has been the impact on the group of each member taking on a specialist role? Think back to your group's collaboration skills from the start of the unit. Has taking on specialist roles changed the team's ability to make decisions and resolve conflicts? Did it affect how well you functioned as a team?

Language support

Phrases to support group discussion:

- 'That's an interesting idea; have you thought about...?'

- 'I understand that you're concerned about...; what do you suggest we do about it?'

- 'We've had some great ideas; can anyone see a solution that would be an effective compromise?'

Discussing information and developing understanding

Skills focus
✓ Communication

Learning focus
- Listen to ideas and explore information relevant to a task.
- Actively participate in discussions to achieve an outcome.

Big question: How can we design the best transport system for a location?

Getting started

a) How do you prefer to get around, assuming it's too far to walk?

b) Why do you personally prefer this mode of transport?

c) Compare your notes with a partner – what influences them?

Exploring

Welcome to Collins Island. The population is small, and people have until now travelled by walking or using off-road vehicles. However, current investment in the island means the population is set to increase from a few hundred to several thousand. A sharp rise in tourist numbers is also expected. A new transport system is a priority development for the island. It will provide access to health and education services as well as employment and retail activities.

The island is 8 km from North to South, and 5 km from East to West; it is relatively flat. The key locations are:

- Town A – the largest settlement and home to the hospital and college

- Port B – all visitors arrive at and depart from the ferry terminal; it is also the island's main industrial area

- Village C

- Town D – the island's second largest town

- Village E.

Your team will be making recommendations about a suitable transport system for Collins Island. You will each be working in the same specialist roles from Unit 3.1, to allow for a full range of perspectives to be considered.

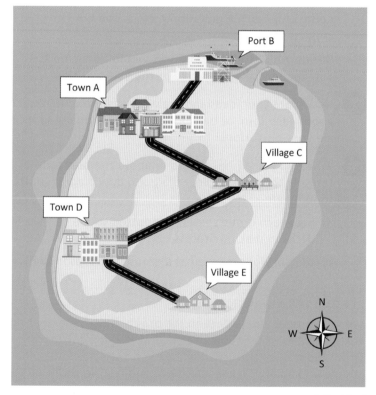

Collins Island

2 **a)** Focusing on your own specialist role, make notes about what you think will be important to consider when looking at the Collins Island transport system.

b) Share your ideas within your team. Together develop a list of essential requirements for the transport system. Make sure that *all* group members contribute to the discussion.

The island government has received three submissions about possible transport systems. The system must not use **internal combustion engines** and must be **self-funding**.

3 Read through the details of the three submissions below. Copy and complete the PMI grid below, to gather your thoughts about each option.

	Plus (+) features	Minus (–) features	Interesting points
Option A: Cycles and cycle paths			
Option B: Trams			
Option C: Driverless cars			

Option A: surfaced cycle paths with cycles for hire, bicycle rickshaws with drivers providing a taxi service and cargo bikes for goods deliveries. The cost of building the paths will be covered by the hire charges for the bikes, and the rickshaw and cargo bike fees. Bikes can be hired in towns and villages. Paths will be narrow and traffic single file.

Hire bikes.

Bicycle rickshaw.

Cargo bike.

Option B: a tramline with **automated** driverless trams; the trams will have goods **compartments** for parcels and boxes. The cost of building and running the system is covered by the fares. The electric trams are powered by solar cells and depart every 20 minutes from Town A and Village E.

Option C: existing paths will be upgraded to roads and driverless cars installed. These electric cars will be summoned by smartphone and paid for by passengers as they ride. As the seats fold down, they can also be used to carry light goods. The cars run on electricity generated by large solar panels linked to charging points, where cars charge up when not in use. The roads are narrow, and all cars will run at the same speed, so there will be no overtaking. Cars return to the **depot** at Port B for storage.

Developing

The government of Collins Island needs to decide which of the transport systems would be the most suitable. Each of the organisations presenting plans has agreed to send a representative to respond to questions as part of a **consultation**.

> ### Vocabulary
>
> **depot**: place where buses, trains or other vehicles are stored when not in use
>
> **consultation**: formal process of discussion in order to arrive at a decision

4 In your specialist role, think up some questions to ask each organisation. Sort these into three lists, one for each planned system. Some questions could apply to two or even all three proposals.

5 Look at the two samples sets of questions below. They have been written in role as the Inclusion Manager.

    a) Working on your own, consider the strengths and weaknesses of each list.

Sample answer A:

> • How will your system cope with wheelchairs?
>
> • How will your system cope with pushchairs (or strollers)?
>
> • How will your system work for people on crutches?

Sample answer B:

> • *How will you make sure that your system is accessible to a wide range of people?*
>
> • *What physical mobility issues can your system accommodate?*
>
> • *How will payments, ticketing and signage work for people who have hearing and/or sight impairments?*

    b) Discuss your ideas in pairs, then feed back to the class. Come up with a class checklist for effective questions.

    c) Now, return to your three lists of questions. Can you improve them based on the class checklist?

Final task

As part of the consultation for the Collins Island transport system, three organisations have raised the following objections.

Organisation	Feedback
Disabled Action	Option A isn't practical for wheelchair users. Option B will work if the stations have raised platforms that can be accessed by ramps. Option C might work if the cars can accommodate a wheelchair and have ramps.
Friends of the Soil	We object to options B and C due to the negative environmental impact of building tracks or roads and of manufacturing rechargeable batteries.
Taxpayers Club	We agree the transport system should be paid for by users. However, options B and C use expensive technologies, so fares will be too high.

6 Consider these objections working in your original group (with people of different specialist roles). In your role, consider:

a) Do you have any questions about any of the objections?

b) Have any of the objections caused you to re-think the options?

7 Now, return to your specialist group (the group in which you are all doing the same role).

a) Discuss your reaction to each of the transport options (bikes, trams and driverless cars). For each option, produce a list of bullet points under three headings:

Why this option should be supported	Why this option should be opposed	Further questions that need to be asked

Refer to listening and negotiation skills in the 'Checklist for success' to support your discussion.

b) To what extent did your specialist group agree about the three options? How did you manage to resolve any areas of disagreement? Make notes on how well you communicated within your group, identifying any areas for improvement.

Checklist for success

✔ Express your ideas clearly, explaining the reasoning.

✔ Listen to other people's reasons, then look for areas of agreement you can build on.

✔ If the group can't agree, take a group vote. Group members on the losing side might then disengage, so look for ways of keeping them involved.

❷ REFLECTION POINT

In this activity, you have worked on your own, in a specialist group and in a general group. You have also responded to objections from pressure groups. Reflect on these ways of working.

• Which has worked best for you and why?

• Which has been less helpful and why?

• Would you like to see any changes in these ways of working? Give details.

Recommending action to address an issue

Skills focus
✓ Analysis
Learning focus
• Explore an issue at a national and global level.
• Recommend and justify a course of action designed to address the issue.

Big question: What problems does transport have to solve as well as moving people around?

Getting started

One problem you might have identified in relation to transportation is the emission of greenhouse gases; it makes a significant contribution to climate change.

1 a) Working with a partner, create a flow diagram to summarise the impact of transportation on climate change. Aim to use key terminology in your diagram.

   b) Share your flow charts with the class. Discuss the best ways to summarise the relationship between transportation and climate change visually.

> In Stage 8, you looked at other examples of greenhouse gas (GHG) emissions leading to climate change. Remind yourself of these examples and the key terminology.

Exploring

To better understand how transportation links to the issue of climate change, you have been asked to review three data sources as part of the Collins Island consultation.

2 a) What does the data in Figure 3.3.1 show in general? Write a sentence to summarise the information.

   b) What percentage of **direct** and **indirect** GHG emissions is transportation responsible for?

3 Now consider Figure 3.3.2 showing GHG emissions for different economic sectors since 1990.

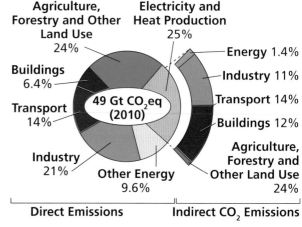

Figure 3.3.1: GHG emissions by economic sector.

Agriculture, Forestry and Other Land Use 24%
Electricity and Heat Production 25%
Buildings 6.4%
Transport 14%
Industry 21%
Other Energy 9.6%

49 Gt CO₂eq (2010)

Energy 1.4%
Industry 11%
Transport 14%
Buildings 12%
Agriculture, Forestry and Other Land Use 24%

Direct Emissions   Indirect CO₂ Emissions

Source: Intergovernmental Panel on Climate Change (IPCC), 2022.

Figure 3.3.2: GHG emissions by economic sector since 1990

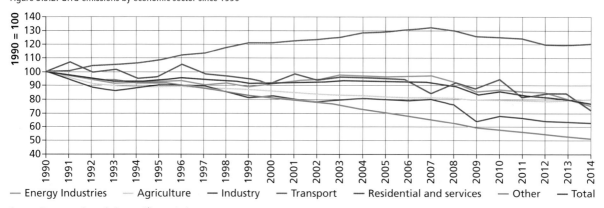

— Energy Industries   — Agriculture   — Industry   — Transport   — Residential and services   — Other   — Total

Source: European Commission on Climate Action.

a) Write a sentence to summarise what the graph shows.

b) What does the graph show about GHG linked to transport?

c) Taking the 1990 level as 100, what is the 2014 level of GHG from transport?

Figure 3.3.3 shows GHG emissions made by different types of vehicles on a journey between two cities.

Figure 3.3.3: Transport emissions.

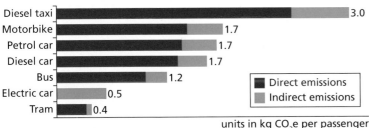

units in kg CO_2e per passenger

Source: UK Department for Transport, 2021.

Vocabulary

direct emissions: those released by the vehicle during use

indirect emissions: emissions from the production of the fuel

4 Working with a partner, discuss these questions:

a) Why is pollution measured in kg CO_2e per passenger?

b) Which vehicles emit the most and least pollution?

c) Why are bus emissions less than those from a car?

d) Suggest why the emissions from an electric car are all indirect.

e) Are indirect emissions less damaging than direct emissions? Why?

5 Return to your original group (of four different specialists).

a) Agree a summary of what the data shows for inclusion in the consultation. Write this down.

b) What arguments should be put forward to justify why the island's planners should consider GHG emissions when designing their transport system? Make a list.

c) Later, you will present your ideas and make a recommendation. Which graphic would best convince the planners to look at transport in a more sustainable way? Explain your choice.

Developing

Another important aspect to consider when planning a transport system is future demand – what might demand for the system be in, say, 10 or 20 years? It's not much good planning a system based on current demand if that demand is set to increase considerably.

These three scenarios suggest how the island may have changed in 10 years' time. They are intended to help the island's planners consider how 'future proof' each transport system is.

- Scenario 1: The island population doubles. Towns and villages have grown to accommodate the increased population.

- Scenario 2: The development of the island's **horticulture** means farms are producing much larger quantities of fruit and vegetables; this needs to be transported to the towns and villages, and to the port for export.

- Scenario 3: The impact of climate change on the island has resulted in hotter summers, colder and wetter winters, and more storms. This has led to more frequent periods of drought and flooding.

6 Working in your group, discuss each transport system in relation to each scenario. How easy or difficult would it be to modify each system to deal with these changes?

   a) Copy and complete the chart below to record your group's ideas.

	Option A: Bikes	Option B: Trams	Option C: Driverless cars
Scenario 1: Island population doubles			
Scenario 2: Increased horticulture production			
Scenario 3: Increased drought and flooding			

   b) Using your notes, explain:

   - which transport option would be able to cope best with a significant increase in passenger numbers

   - which option would be most easily adapted for a large growth in horticulture production

   - which option would be able to cope best with a changing climate.

Here are two sample arguments based on scenario 1 – the island population doubles.

7 Working on your own, make notes on the strengths and weaknesses of each argument. Then discuss your ideas within your group.

A:

If demand increases significantly, the bike system will get clogged up and slow down. The trams will cope best because the trains will be made longer, and double track can be built to increase capacity. The cars will cope to a point because more can be added, but eventually this system will clog up as well.

B:

Increased passenger numbers will mean more bicycles, more tram seats and more driverless cars. The tram system can probably cope with this best because there will be the options of longer and more frequent trains. The driverless cars will cope up to the point where the routes are full and more roads are needed. The bicycle system may struggle more because the users determine the flow; if it's busier, wider paths will be needed.

Final task

8 You have now explored the three transport options, considered your own 'expert opinion' as a specialist and explored issues such as climate change, carbon emissions and how 'future-proof' each option is. You will now work in your original group of four specialists to make a recommendation as to which transport option will be best for Collins Island. You will share and justify your recommendation in a poster presentation.

a) Make notes to plan your group's poster, which will draw together and summarise your ideas. Consider:

- Which transport system does your group recommend?

- What are the most persuasive arguments for choosing that transport option?

- Why are the other two proposed transport options less convincing?

Make sure that your arguments:

- draw on the specialist perspectives of everyone in the group

- include reference to environmental impacts and adaptability in the face of future change.

b) When you are clear and in agreement on the key arguments, prepare a poster summarising and justifying your group's decisions. You can use the phrasing in the Language support box to help you.

9 Display your poster and look at the posters other groups have prepared. For each poster:

a) Identify any strong and effective features. For example, which arguments does your group find persuasive?

b) Decide if any aspects of the poster were less convincing and why.

Summarise your group's feedback on a sticky note below the poster.

Language support

'Our preferred option would be…'

'The reason for this is…'

'This is supported by…'

'Another key factor we considered was…'

❓ REFLECTION POINT

- How well do you think your group identified a solution that will address the issue of transport and climate change?

- What other issues were you trying to get the transport solution for Collins Island to address? How well do you think your group achieved this?

Reflecting on how a team can improve and succeed

Skills focus
✓ Reflection
Learning focus
• Consider the benefits and challenges of teamwork.
• Reflect on group outcomes achieved and identify targets for improvement.

Big question: What is the best way of using a team to make an impression?

Getting started

1 What do you think are the benefits and challenges of working in a team, based on your experience from the activities in this chapter? Think about:

a) the workload for each team member compared with working individually

b) how well team members understand the tasks to be done

c) how well team members cope with people having different opinions

d) how easy it is to organise the team so the task gets done

e) how easy it is to agree roles within the team.

Discuss your ideas with a partner, then feedback to the class.

Exploring

Your task in this unit is to give a group presentation on your recommendation for the Collins Island transport system. You can use your group's poster from Unit 3.3 as a plan for the content of the presentation.

The presentation needs to be planned and then given as a team, so you will need to think carefully how best to utilise everyone.

2 In your group, discuss your initial ideas for how you will work together as a team to create and then give the presentation.

a) How will you make good use of the specialist roles of the team members?

b) How will you prepare and present the work so that it is clear it is a collaborative effort?

c) How will you deal with any differences in the points of view of team members?

Make notes to record the results of your discussion to return to later.

Consider the sample plan presented a series of slides on the next page.

Slide 1 – introduces team, with pictures of team members. Each team member stands up and says what their specialist role was. →	Slide 2 – sets the context of the Collins Island transport system, showing the map and explaining the challenge. →	Slide 3 – presents our proposal, clearly stating why we are recommending the tram system. ↓
Slide 6 – gives reasons why the other two options are not as good in our opinion. ←	Slide 5 – summarises the limitations of our chosen transport option. ←	Slide 4 – gives the reasons why we are backing our chosen transport option.

Then read through the sample feedback:

Why do we need Slide 2? – we all know what the challenge is.

I like the way you're recognising in Slide 5 that the best solution isn't necessarily perfect.

Why not have a slide for each of the specialist areas?

You should merge slides 3 and 4 so that you explain the reasoning at the same time as the decision.

3 Working on your own, read the plan and the comments carefully.

a) Take each comment in turn and write a brief response to it, indicating whether you agree and why.

b) Make a note of:

- any other feedback you want to add about the plan

- any of the points in the plan you want to use in your team's presentation.

Developing

A slide deck could be used to share ideas. Look at this sample slide.

We recommend the bicycle system.

Advantages:	Disadvantages:
✔ No pollution ✔ Cycling is a great way to keep fit ✔ Building cycle paths causes less damage than roads or rail tracks ✔ Hire bikes are collected from and returned to racks – so no staff costs ✔ People with disabilities, the elderly and children can be carried in rickshaws ✔ Goods can be carried in cargo bikes ✔ If usage increases, more bikes can be provided	✗ If it's raining, you get wet! ✗ Rickshaws can be expensive, as each driver can only carry a few people ✗ Cargo bikes can only carry a limited amount of goods

Overall:

- This is a low-cost solution, requiring few staff and keeping the islanders fit.
- The initial investment is much lower than trams or cars.
- The system can easily cope with changing demand.

4 Working in your group, evaluate the slide content. Copy and complete the table below to structure your feedback.

Has the team...	How well has the team achieved this outcome?	Targets for improvement
a) considered a range of factors?		
b) made good use of their specialist insights?		
c) suggested how limitations could be overcome?		
d) used images to support understanding or create impact?		

Here are two sets of notes that look at the slide content and consider how well it made use of specialist insights.

A:

> The Inclusion Manager has identified how accessible the system is for people with disabilities and the Environmental Protection Officer has referred to the lack of pollution. The Accountant has talked about keeping the initial outlay down, but I can't see much input from the Sales Manager.

B:

> The Accountant has referred to low initial costs but hasn't indicated much about how income generated will cover maintenance and renewal to provide a long-term future. The Inclusion Manager has talked about what the provision is but not how well they think it will work. There's little there about how to maximise sales apart from pointing out it will keep people fit. The Environmental Protection Officer has referred to lack of pollution but does not consider the negative impact of construction.

5 Working on your own, consider each of the comments in turn.

a) Which are likely to be useful to the team in improving their work?

b) Which are less useful?

As part of the final task for this unit, you will be giving feedback on another group's presentation.

6 **a)** Work in your group to create a checklist of the key features to look for in the other group's presentation. This will be useful in keeping your feedback relevant. For example, you might note down:

Each point made had supporting evidence.

The diagrams were clearly visible and relevant.

b) Now think about presentation skills when giving a presentation and create a checklist to use when observing the other group's presentation. For example, you might include:

Presenters spoke clearly and projected their voice.

Presenters used slide content as prompts and didn't simply read from them.

The whole team was involved in the presentation.

Final task

7 **a)** Prepare and give your group's presentation on the Collins Island transport system. Then watch and listen to the other group's presentation.

b) Present the other group with their feedback and respond to any questions they may have. Then listen to the feedback of the other group on your presentation. Check understanding of any points you are unclear about.

Use the checklists you created to:

- prepare for and organise your own presentation

- record feedback to give to the other group.

8 Working on your own, write a short reflective piece of around 150 words on how well your group worked together to:

a) create and give a presentation

b) feed back to the other group on its presentation.

Draw on your own self-assessment as well as the other group's feedback. Include examples of how well your group:

- came up with useful ideas

- examined the ideas put forward and suggested how to use them

- coordinated and managed the work

- provided and listened to feedback.

❓ REFLECTION POINT

You should now have a good sense of how well your group works as a team. You should also be developing a sense of your own individual contribution. Note down:

- how well you participated in the group and contributed to the group outcome

- ways in which you could have worked more effectively to enable the group to complete the task well.

Explaining how exploring different perspectives changes minds

Skills focus
✓ Reflection
Learning focus
- Reflect on how your own perspectives may have changed.
- Consider how exploring different perspectives led to these changes.

Big question: When is it OK for an expert to change their mind?

Getting started

In this chapter, you have been looking at transport and comparing different transport options using specialist perspectives.

Here are some people boarding a bus. This is part of the local transport provision. It is powered by a diesel engine and links the outer parts of a town with the centre. The service is funded by fares and the frequency of the bus service is determined by demand, which is reviewed every six months.

1 Drawing on the skills and understanding you have developed in this chapter, complete a PMI (Plus, Minus, Interesting) grid about whether a bus service operated in this way is likely to be good.

2 Think about the way you approached this task. Has the work you have done in this chapter developed your ability to produce a quality response? Consider this on your own, then share your ideas with a partner. Make some notes to share with the class.

Exploring

Look at the images of the rapid transit system at Miami International Airport in the USA. Its function is to move people and their luggage quickly and easily from one terminal to another. There are no tickets; passengers just board and leave.

The rapid transit system at Miami International Airport.

Here are some people's reactions to this form of transport:

> This is a poor design from the business point of view. No tickets! That's a missed opportunity! It means it's bound to run at a loss. People should pay to ride.

> This is great from the accessibility perspective – wide doors, no steps and plenty of rails. Great for luggage trolleys, pushchairs and wheelchairs.

> It's powered by electric motors, but I want to know where the electricity is coming from.

3 Working as a group, consider these reactions and compose responses to them.

a) Do you agree with any of these points? If so, why? If not, what do you take issue with? Is anything in the point valid or worth further exploration?

b) Share your group's responses with the class and listen to what others think. Has anyone else come up with ideas that would make you change your mind or modify your views?

4 Working on your own, consider and note down your responses to these questions:

a) If you change your mind about something after listening to other people, why is that? Do any of these make a difference?

- Someone who has more information than me and knows something I don't.

- Someone who argues more passionately.

- Someone who has a different perspective because of their experience.

b) Sometimes people who argue very passionately for or against something don't have much evidence to support their case. Suggest an effective way of dealing with this.

Developing

Dania has recently arrived on Collins Island. She has a job in a florist shop, making up floral displays for special events. The island's population is growing and there's plenty of business. The consultation about the new transport system is in full flow and everyone has an opinion; no decision has yet been made. Everyone who comes into the shop wants to know what she thinks – and to tell her what they think!

Dania listens carefully to what everyone says and then makes a note of how she can see each of the three transport options affecting her, both as an individual and for her work.

5 Read through Dania's notes in the table on the next page. Reflect on your responses to these questions:

a) Are the points she makes valid?

b) Have they caused you to reconsider the three transport options in any way?

Make notes to record your responses.

Options	Positive features	Features that are problematic
Cycle system	I like the idea of being able to cycle everywhere – a great way to keep fit. The cargo bikes will be a great way of delivering flowers.	If the weather is bad, cycling may not be as easy. It will be important that the hire costs are not high. We'd like to have our own cargo bike for the business, but I'm not sure that will be allowed.
Trams	This will be a smooth way of getting around the island in all weathers and will avoid congestion.	I think the trams may work better for people than goods – delivering flowers this way may not be as easy.
Driverless cars	These will be a quick way of getting around and should work well in all weathers. The cars are big enough to work well for carrying flowers.	I worry about the availability of cars at busy times. If it's raining and lots of people are wanting to travel, it could be hard to get hold of a car. Customers don't like to be kept waiting.

Dania has been talking to several other small business owners. Several of them are quite worried about some aspects of the transport plans. They feel that these have been drawn up thinking more about individual passengers than the needs of businesses that are dependent on goods being transported quickly and easily to a variety of destinations.

'I deliver parcels containing goods that have been bought online. Most of the packages are not very big but people expect them to arrive promptly.'

'I'm a plumber and need to get to people's homes to fix problems with the pipes. Are any of these plans going to work for me? I need to get around quickly and have tools and materials with me.'

'I run a takeaway food business in Town A. People all over the island buy from me and sometimes they need me to deliver the meals. They expect them to be delivered promptly and to be hot!'

6 In your original group of four specialists, consider the reactions of Dania and the three small business owners to the proposals. Discuss:

a) Have these comments caused you to change your mind about your group's recommendation? Why?

b) Have these comments made you aware of any additional selling points for the different transport options?

c) Why is it important to talk to a wide range of people during a consultation?

Final task

This final task is a reflection on how your personal perspective on the Collins Island transport system has changed as a result of exploring different perspectives.

7 Working with a new partner, interview each other using these questions:

a) In what ways did you change your perspective on the Collins Island transport system?

b) What made you change your mind?

8 Now, write a reflective piece of 150–200 words in which you:

- consider your initial perspective on the Collins Island transport system

- identify key ways in which your perspective changed

- explain what caused you to change your mind.

You might consider the following influences:

- other people in your group

- taking on a specialist role

- exploring environmental and accessibility factors in more depth

- the perspectives of small business owners.

> During the interview, make notes while your partner is speaking, to share with them later – so they can draw on them when writing their reflection.

❓ REFLECTION POINT

Consider these points of view. Which do you agree with and why?

- 'Listening to different perspectives doesn't change your point of view – it just gives you reasons to believe in what you already thought.'

- 'Listening to different perspectives always reveals something new – it makes you see something in a new light.'

Applying what you have learned

Your task

> Your reputation as a transport consultant has spread and you have been invited to judge competing bids for the contract to design and construct a river crossing. You will need to make a judgement and respond to interview questions. The unsuccessful bidders are likely to be disappointed and will want to know why you made the decision you did.
>
> Working on your own, draw upon your experience of comparing bids against a range of criteria.

Approaching the task

1. Reviewing your work so far

Earlier in this chapter, you evaluated three competing bids to provide a transport system (bikes, trams or driverless cars) for Collins Island.

a) Think back to the work you did on the Collins Island transport system. List the key aspects of making a good decision.

b) Now, look at this sample response and see how it compares with your ideas. To what extent do you agree or disagree with their choices? Note down your ideas.

> I think the three most important aspects to making a good decision were:
>
> ✔ Considering each proposal carefully – listening to all the arguments rather than making a snap decision and then having to defend it.
>
> ✔ Having a set of criteria that could be applied to each bid, so we were fair in what we were looking for.
>
> ✔ Being prepared to compromise; none of the bids was perfect so we had to decide what was most important.

2. Considering the river crossing proposals

A national government is planning to install a new river crossing in its capital city. The river runs through the middle of the city and thousands of people cross from one side to the other each day.

There are bridges over the river, but they become congested at busy times and people sometimes must queue for a long time to cross. The mayor of the city wants a crossing that is eye-catching and will excite visitors. They have visited the Docklands Cable Car in London, which crosses the River Thames, the Golden Gate Bridge in San Francisco, and the Star Ferries in Hong Kong. Whatever is built must attract interest and stimulate visitor numbers while also getting thousands of people from one side of the river to the other each day.

The three proposals are:

Proposal A: Cable cars will run from stations at either side of the river along aerial cables. Each car takes ten passengers and can accommodate wheelchairs. It has a capacity of 2500 passengers per hour and the crossing takes 5 minutes. It is powered by electric motors and the power can be supplied in a variety of ways. It will provide stunning views over the city and will be clearly visible from miles around.

Proposal B: A bridge will run from bank to bank carrying vehicles, bicycles and pedestrians. It will take about 5 minutes to cross by vehicle, though this time will increase during busy periods, and around 40 minutes to cross by foot. As the transition to electric vehicles takes place over the next few years, the bridge will need no modification. It will be a striking landmark.

Proposal C: A small fleet of ferries will run from bank to bank. Each ferry will be able to carry over 700 passengers and make the crossing in 10 minutes, though additional time will be taken boarding and leaving the boats, especially during busy periods. The boats take a limited number of bicycles but no vehicles. They are powered by internal combustion engines that can run on sustainable fuel such as vegetable oil.

Working as a group:

a) Brainstorm questions that occur to you having read the proposals.

b) From these questions, list potential criteria – for example, appearance, cost, sustainability, capacity to respond to changing demand – against which the proposals could be evaluated.

3. Developing a set of criteria

Working on your own, decide up to 10 criteria against which to judge the river crossing bids.

Look at the following sample criteria.

Factors	Score out of 10		
	Cable car	Bridge	Ferry
Accessible to old, young and infirm			
Looks cool			
Is green			
Can charge to use			
Quick to cross			

a) Working in a small group, discuss the strengths and weaknesses of this set of criteria.

b) Now draw up your own set of criteria against which to judge the river crossing bids. You can have up to a maximum of 10 criteria.

To help in your evaluation, you could use a weighting system in which the more important criteria carry double or triple points. Here is one possibility.

Factor	Weighting	Cable car score (out of 10)	Weighted score
Attractive appearance	1	8	8
Ease of use	3	6	18
Sustainability	2	6	12
Adjusts well to changing demand	2	4	8

c) In a small group, discuss this scoring system and how well it can be justified.

d) Decide whether you will add a weighting system to your own set of criteria; if you do, add it against your criteria. Note down the reasons for your decision.

4. Reaching and justifying an overall decision

Working on your own, judge each of the three river crossing proposals. Use the 'Checklist for success' to help you. Record your decisions and reasoning in full.

> **Checklist for success**
>
> ✔ Apply and weight the criteria you have decided upon equally and fairly.
>
> ✔ Identify the strengths and weaknesses of each proposal, as reflected by the overall scores.
>
> ✔ Come to a clear decision.
>
> ✔ Explain how you have reached your decision, so that everyone can see it was fair and led to the best decision for the city.

5. Preparing for the interview

When presenting your decision about the river crossing bid, you will also take questions about how you arrived at your conclusion. Working on your own, note down your responses to these questions:

a) When you are looking at a proposal for a new transport system, what do you think are the most important things to look at?

b) Why do you think it is important to look at a proposal from several different perspectives?

c) Since you have been working in this area, how have your views changed about what is important in a good transport plan?

d) Give an example of a proposal you have studied where you ended up changing your mind about it the more you looked at it.

6. The interviews

Working in a small group, take turns at interviewing each other. Make notes on how well each of you presented and justified your ideas. When all interviews are complete, share feedback.

Reflecting on your progress

In this chapter you have made and justified decisions about alternative solutions to transport problems – as part of a group for the Collins Island transport activity, and on your own for the river crossings bids.

Reflect on what you found easy and what was more challenging when working in a group and individually.

Check your progress

Beginning	Developing	Going beyond
• I can work in a team, taking on a specialist role and making contributions.	• I can function effectively in a team, adopt both general and specialist roles and make a range of contributions.	• I can function in a team in a range of roles, contributing ideas and developing other people's contributions.
• I can gather information and suggest how it helps to address an issue.	• I can gather information systematically and organise it to structure a response to an issue.	• I can gather information systematically and use it to develop a range of responses to an issue.
• I can suggest how things I've found out have encouraged me to think again about an issue.	• I can reflect on how things I've explored have given me a broader perspective on an issue.	• I can reflect on ideas developed through exploring issues in greater depth and use these to evaluate different approaches to an issue.
• I can reflect on how well I've worked with the rest of the team and suggest how I might improve on this.	• I can reflect on my role in the team, the effectiveness of the team and identify areas for improvement.	• I can critically reflect on how well the team has worked, how effective my collaboration skills are and identify areas for improvement.

Next steps

Find opportunities to participate in groups or committees and see what kind of contribution would help the group to function more effectively.

When gathering information about an issue, look for evidence to support a different view and use it to test your own thinking.

When exploring an issue in depth, look for multiple independent sources to build a stronger evidence base.

Communicating ideas: improving your writing skills

Sport and recreation

4

Sporting competitions excite fans the world over, as they follow global tournaments like the football World Cup or cricket's Indian Premier League.

Many people actively participate in sports, perhaps in competitive teams or a game of table tennis in the local park. This is great fun, and it also makes us fit and healthy.

In this chapter, you will explore the topic of 'Sport and recreation', thinking about the following issues:

- **How important is physical activity for school children?**

- **What are the consequences of children's lack of exercise?**

- **How can we make walking and cycling easier and safer?**

- **How do you know which reference sources you can rely on?**

- **How do you persuade people to take action?**

- **What role does government have over individual decisions?**

You will be developing a range of collaboration and research skills:

4.1 Using and presenting research findings

4.2 Explaining causes and consequences

4.3 Explaining the strengths and weaknesses of arguments

4.4 Evaluating and referencing sources and evidence

4.5 Proposing a course of action

4.6 Applying what you have learned

4.7 Giving a personal response.

Your final task will be to work in a group to create an entry into a national competition. The competition is to create a scheme for young people to be more active. You are going to propose a walking and cycling strategy for your school.

Using and presenting research findings

Skills focus
✓ Communication
✓ Analysis
Learning focus
• Identify perspectives and synthesise arguments and evidence.
• Present relevant, well-reasoned and clearly structured arguments.

Big question: How important is physical activity for school children?

Getting started

1 Read the following extract, which is taken from a global study.

The first ever global trends for adolescent insufficient physical activity show that urgent action is needed to increase physical activity levels in girls and boys aged 11 to 17 years. The study, published in *The Lancet Child and Adolescent Health* journal and produced by researchers from the World Health Organization (WHO), finds that more than 80 per cent of school-going adolescents globally did not meet current recommendations of at least one hour of physical activity per day – including 85 per cent of girls and 78 per cent of boys.

Source: World Health Organization, November 2019.

Discuss the extract with a partner, considering the following points:

a) What did the study reveal about the physical activity levels of 11–17-year-olds?

b) What are the current requirements for physical activity?

c) Do you and your partner meet these levels? Why/why not?

d) Why do you think there is a difference between boys and girls? Why might this be the case?

Exploring

The above study by the World Health Organization (WHO) found that most young people are not sufficiently physically active. The study argues that this lack of activity could cause problems for their current and future health.

So why are young people across the world taking less exercise than is recommended? Here are some comments:

> During the week, I'm just too busy with school. At the weekend, I'm tired, so I tend to watch television or play games online with my friends.

> I live in the city, nowhere near a place like a park for running or sport, so I don't really have opportunities for doing more exercise.

> None of my friends is really into sport and I can't go out and do stuff on my own, so I don't bother about it.

2 **a)** From these statements, list the obstacles that might prevent regular exercise.

b) In a group, discuss your list and add any other factors you can think of which make it difficult for children to be active.

c) Write a summary paragraph of your findings. You could begin:

> There are several factors that affect children's participation in regular physical exercise...

d) Looking at your summary, consider whether the results of the WHO study are likely to be confirmed in your own country. Explain your reasoning.

Many countries have started to encourage school children to walk or cycle to school to ensure they have some daily activity.

3 **a)** With a quick show of hands around the class, see how many ways everyone makes their way to and from school. Make a note of the most popular methods.

b) Write down the results of your class survey in simple form. For example:

Walking	Bicycle	Tram	Private car	School bus	Public bus
5	8	1	3	9	5

In this chapter, you will be comparing your school with other schools around the world.

Graphs and charts can be a useful way of presenting data to make it easily comprehensible. A bar chart and pie chart for the different ways of getting to school could look like this:

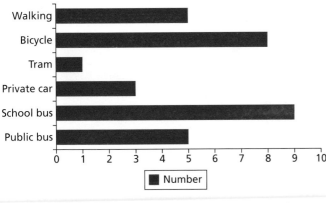

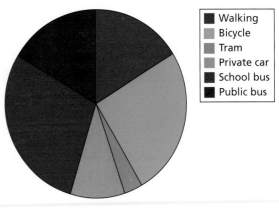

c) Which chart do you think is the more effective way of presenting the data? Why?

d) Now use the data for your class to **extrapolate** what the figures might be for your whole school. When doing this, you will need to account for any **modifying factors** such as the weather at different times of year and the age of students.

e) Do you think the results would be the same in other schools? Would they be the same in other countries? Discuss these questions with a partner, then share your view with the class.

> **Vocabulary**
>
> **extrapolate**: work out from evidence, assuming its indications will remain consistent
>
> **modifying factors**: factors that will create changes in the data

You are now going to test your ideas by conducting the same survey with one class in each year group, or even throughout the school.

4 In your group, choose one of the following questions. Design and conduct a survey that will give you information to recognise trends:

- How many students walk or cycle to school in the different year groups of the school?

- How are the numbers of walkers/cyclists affected by the weather?

- How are the numbers of walkers/cyclists affected by the time of year?

- How are the numbers of walkers/cyclists affected by the distance they must travel?

From your survey results, you should be able to analyse how students' choices are affected by their age, the weather and the distance they have to travel. These trends would give useful information for any advice or proposal to encourage greater participation in walking and cycling.

5 Present your results in text and appropriate charts, thinking back to what you decided about the list, bar chart and pie chart.

6 What factors do you think will influence how students in different countries get to school? Discuss your ideas with your group and write a list of suggestions.

Developing

You are probably aware that exercise is good for you. But what does the research say?

7 **a)** Read the following source texts. What benefits of walking and cycling do these articles describe? Work with a partner to make notes.

b) Write a paragraph to synthesise the two sources and explain their findings. Use the vocabulary in the 'Language support' box.

Language support

When presenting your results, use phrases that refer to your charts, such as:

'The survey results indicate that...'

'The chart clearly demonstrates that...'

'The graph suggests that...'

Language support

- Use words and phrases such as: shows, demonstrates, indicates, suggests, tells us that.

- Useful words for comparison: similarly, like, as, also, likewise.

- Useful words for contrast: unlike, in contrast to, however, whereas, but.

Health benefits of walking

You carry your own body weight when you walk. This is known as weight-bearing exercise. Some of the benefits include:

- increased cardiovascular and pulmonary (heart and lung) fitness
- reduced risk of heart disease and stroke
- improved management of conditions such as hypertension (high blood pressure), high cholesterol, joint and muscular pain or stiffness, and diabetes
- stronger bones and improved balance
- increased muscle strength and **endurance**
- reduced body fat.

Source: *Better Health Channel*, 'Walking for good health', Department of Health, State Government of Victoria, Australia.

Why cycling is great for your legs, lungs, immune system and mind

by Michelle Arthurs-Brennan

If you're considering joining the world of cycling, here are some good reasons to get on your bike this year.

1. Cycling improves mental well-being
2. Strengthen your immune system by cycling
3. Cycling can help you lose weight
4. Cycling builds muscle
5. Cyclists have better lung health
6. Cycling cuts heart disease and cancer risk
7. Cycling is low impact
8. Cyclists sleep better
9. Cycling boosts your brain power
10. Cycling improves **spatial awareness**

Source: *Cycling Weekly* online magazine, 16 August 2022.

Final task

8. In your group, make a poster or short video explaining the advantages of walking and cycling to school.

   - Draw on the evidence from your research to back up your points. The poster could include the charts you made earlier.

   - Use the language techniques for presenting information and arguments.

   Key points to include:

   ✔ The benefits of walking and cycling to students and the local community.

   ✔ Barriers to walking and cycling that might need to be overcome – with suggestions.

   ✔ Ways of making walking and cycling easier and more enjoyable for everyone.

Vocabulary

endurance: ability to continue with a difficult or painful activity over a long period of time

spatial awareness: ability to judge the relationships between objects, both stationary and moving, in the environment

You could allocate the roles in your group like this:

1. Pull together the research and introduce the topic.

2. Discuss the issue from your local perspective.

3. Compare the local perspective with the global issue.

4. Conclude and recommend a course of action.

❓ REFLECTION POINT

Have the evidence and surveys changed your perspective on walking or cycling to school? If you were to walk or cycle to school, what difficulties might you encounter and what opportunities might there be?

Explaining causes and consequences

Skills focus

✓ Analysis

Learning focus

- Identify patterns and trends in graphical and numerical data to support your argument or perspective.
- Make links between causes and consequences of the issue at personal, local and global levels.

Big question: What are the consequences of children's lack of exercise?

Getting started

1   Working in a small group, discuss your favourite leisure activity and how you like to relax at the weekend.

   a) How many of your suggestions include physical activity?

   b) What is the balance between **sedentary** and physical activities?

2   The WHO survey (in Unit 4.1) found that 85 per cent of girls and 78 per cent of boys do not do enough physical exercise. Do your group's favoured activities help towards the WHO target of an hour's exercise a day? Explain your reasoning.

Exploring

As you saw in the previous unit, there are several reasons why young people might not exercise enough.

3   Read this account about Ivan's experience. Then, working on your own, make some notes about Ivan.

   a) What are Ivan's favourite activities?

   b) What are the causes of Ivan's low levels of physical activity?

   c) What advantages does technology give to Ivan?

   d) What consequences does his use of technology have for him?

> ### Vocabulary
>
> **sedentary**: seated, inactive
>
> **peer pressure**: influence on behaviour that comes from friendship groups

Ivan loves electronic gadgets, particularly his computer and his phone. 'I can get everything I want in a few clicks,' he says. He likes to watch bands and funny clips online and he sometimes streams films to his computer. He is very competitive and plays games online with his friends most evenings and at weekends. 'It's great,' he says; 'I can play and socialise without leaving my bedroom.'

Ivan lives in a large city and the streets are busy with traffic. Both his parents work and are usually very tired when they come home, so he really appreciates keeping in touch with his friends online.

4 **a)** With a partner, discuss what other factors might prevent children from taking as much exercise as is recommended.

b) Copy and complete the table below to score the following suggestions from 1–5 (1 = not very important; 5 = extremely important).

Reason	1	2	3	4	5
Low energy, feeling tired					
Unmotivated, lacking interest					
Lack of available options for activity					
Peer pressure					
Too little time					
Lack of confidence					
Lack of suitable space					
Inappropriate weather or climate					
Preference for other options					

c) Compare your results with others in the class. Can you think of any ways in which some of the problems might be overcome?

Developing

You are now going to consider what the consequences of children's lack of exercise might be.

5 Read Sources A and B, then answer the questions.

Source A:

> The prevalence of overweight and obesity among children and adolescents aged 5–19 has risen dramatically from just 4 per cent in 1975 to just over 18 per cent in 2016. The rise has occurred similarly among both boys and girls: in 2016 18 per cent of girls and 19 per cent of boys were overweight.

Source: Factsheet 'Obesity and overweight', World Health Organization, 2021.

Source B:

> Mental health conditions constitute a major burden of disease for adolescents globally. In 2019, it was estimated that one in seven adolescents experience mental disorders. This amounts to an estimated 166 million adolescents (89 million boys and 77 million girls) globally.

Source: 'Mental health', UNICEF Data, 2021.

a) It is unlikely that a lack of exercise is solely responsible for these trends. Working individually, note down other factors that you think may have contributed to a decline in children's physical and mental health, up to the present day.

b) Discuss your ideas with a partner, and then as a class.

6 Source C is from an online article that lists ten ways in which physical activity helps children develop. Read this extract from the article, which lists three ways, then make notes in response to the questions below.

Source: 'Why is physical activity important for child development?', *Active Health*, Sport Singapore, 2021.

Source C:

10 ways physical activity promotes child development

Physical growth

Exercise, like food, is a fundamental part of a child's physical growth. Exercise helps your child build stronger muscles and bones acting as a stimulus for the body to adapt to. Developing a good physical foundation from a young age includes healthy bone mass and density, which will reduce the risk of developing bone-related diseases such as osteoporosis later on in life.

Refinement of motor skills

For younger children, physical activity during playtime helps with the development

of **motor skills**, which is responsible for helping them master the basic movements they need for everyday life. The development of a child's motor skills means that basic feats such as feeding oneself, tying one's shoelaces and even writing can be attained much faster.

Better posture

Slouching is a common problem in many children and exercise helps to counter this negative trend by improving a child's posture by increasing core and spine strength. Good posture goes a long way

in life – it protects a child's spine from deformation due to excessive slouching and also reduces the chances of experiencing body aches due to bad posture.

a) Who is the target audience of the online article? How can you tell?

b) Find examples of informal and formal language. Why are both styles used?

c) How are each of the points explained and supported?

d) How are examples and suggestions used?

7 a) Using your notes from question 6, try to imitate the style in writing the accompanying paragraphs for two or three of the remaining seven points. The paragraph headings are:

Better fitness

Weight management

Cognitive development

Better mental health

Improved self-esteem

Social skills development

Maintaining cardiovascular health

b) Compare your paragraphs with others in your group. What are the strong points of each? Combine and edit your group's paragraphs to create a final version.

> ### Vocabulary
>
> **motor skills**: the muscle movements developed through practice and repetition in early childhood
>
> **cognitive**: related to thinking and conscious mental processes

8 Read through these figures and the infographic:

- A survey in Hyderabad, India, found that 57 per cent of children walked to school, while only 6 per cent cycled. 36 per cent used some kind of motorised transport, particularly buses.

- In the USA, it is estimated that 12–15% of children walk or cycle to school.

- In the UK, 38% of 11–16-year-olds walk to school, while only 2% of children cycle to school.

- Most children in the UAE take the bus to school.

Sources: 'How do children travel to school in urban India? A cross-sectional study of 5,842 children in Hyderabad' by Shailaja Tetali **et al.**, *BMC Public Health*, 2016; 'Travel to school in California: Findings from the National Household Travel Survey, 2013'; Sustrans survey, September 2021; 'Many UAE children take the bus even if some can walk to school' by Sarwat Nasir, *Khaleej Times*, 11 March 2019.

Mode of travel
Most common modes of travel to school

	Walk	Car	Bus
5-10 years	46%	46%	5%
11-16 years	38%	23%	29%

Trends
Since 2003...

for **primary school children**, the share of car has slightly increased and the share of walking has decreased.

... mode share has remained broadly stable for **secondary school children**.

Source: National Travel Survey factsheet: England 2014, UK Department for Transport.

a) In a sentence or two, write down the causes of low numbers of children cycling to school in all the countries cited.

b) In a sentence or two, write down the causes of higher numbers of children walking to school in India than in the USA, UK and UAE. You will not have complete evidence, but you can make well-based **assumptions**. Try phrases like these:

'It is likely that…because…'

'The cause of…may be that…'

'A probable consequence of…is…'

c) As a class, discuss what you would expect the consequences for children's health to be if the trend shown in the infographic has continued since 2014.

> 🔑 **Key terms**
>
> **et al.**: abbreviation meaning 'and others', used to indicate when a source text has more than one author
>
> **assumption**: something accepted as true without proof

Final task

9 Drawing on all the information in this unit, write a short report about children's physical activity and health.

- Explain how children's inactivity may be connected to the increasing concerns with children's health.

- Explain how regular exercise can be beneficial.

> ❓ REFLECTION POINT
>
> How far do you think that habits acquired as children continue into adult life? If children are encouraged to be more active and become healthier as a result, will the consequence be a more active and healthier adult population in the future?

> It can be useful to divide a report into separate sections, with subheadings, to make the organisation of your ideas clear to the reader. For example, subheadings for this report could be:
>
> 'Background: children's health'
>
> 'The link between inactivity and poor health'
>
> 'The benefits of regular exercise for children'
>
> 'Conclusion'

Explaining the strengths and weaknesses of arguments

Skills focus
✓ Evaluation
Learning focus
- Evaluate a range of sources, considering credibility in terms of factors such as the author, purpose, bias and how well they are supported by other sources.
- Evaluate an argument, considering the structure, reasoning and evidence.

Big question: How can we make walking and cycling easier and safer?

Getting started

So far in this chapter, you have looked at some of the potential benefits of children walking and cycling to school; there have been valid objections, too. You now need to consider all these to form your own judgement.

1 Here are some possible objections and supports; can you add two more points to each list?

Potential objections	Potential supports
• The roads are not safe.	• Children will be fit and healthy.
• There are too many books and other things to carry.	• It will support children's mental health, too.

Exploring

Greenville School, on the edge of a small town, is considering a scheme to encourage students to make their own way to school on foot or by bicycle. It carried out a consultation exercise asking parents for their views. Here are two of the responses.

Parent response A:

'All students who live close to the school should walk or cycle. If the distance between home and school is too great, then other transport may be necessary, but otherwise children would benefit from the exercise. They would be fitter, stronger and in a better mental state for learning. The local area would also be improved as there would be less pollution from the vehicles that would otherwise take them to school. If they walk or cycle, everyone benefits – the students, the school and the local area.'

Parent response B:

'We should not expect children to make their own way to school. As a parent, I want to see that my child gets safely there and safely home again. It is my responsibility. The school bag full of books and equipment is very heavy and my child will be too tired if they have to carry everything to and from school every day. The roads between our house and the school are very busy, so it is not safe to walk or use a bicycle. Even if they did not have an accident crossing a road, they would have to breathe in the fumes every day. My child is much better off in the car.'

key

Central argument of the paragraph

Perspective of writer

Supporting evidence

Acknowledgement of different view

Conclusion

2 Look carefully at the two parent responses and the annotations, then make notes on the following questions:

a) The first parent response refers to 'All students', while the second identifies the writer as a parent, uses the pronoun 'I' and refers to 'my child'. What difference does this make?

b) Both responses provide evidence to support their views. How persuasive is this evidence?

c) Is it important that the parent response A considers that their conclusion might not be suitable for everyone?

d) How effective are the two conclusions? What makes them effective or ineffective?

These questions help you to evaluate the two arguments, to judge which is the more effective. For example, you could start by saying:

Parent A writes in a general way about the benefits of children walking or cycling to school, whereas Parent B clearly identifies their perspective as a parent. By using phrases such as 'I want to see' and referring to 'my child', the second parent presents a narrower perspective and seems less concerned about the broader issues.

Language support

Use adjectives such as these when evaluating evidence:

- Positive: persuasive, convincing, credible, effective, logical, compelling

- Negative: weak, questionable, ineffective, dubious, unconvincing.

e) Note how this example answer uses short quotations to support the judgements made. Continue this paragraph, using your notes on the questions.

Developing

The safety of cycling is a key concern, particularly when cyclists share the road with cars and lorries. An important piece of safety equipment is the helmet, but rules about them vary, and most countries have no laws about them.

You are going to evaluate some of the arguments about the effectiveness of helmets and whether cyclists should be made to wear them.

3 Read this extract, which is written by a journalist and cycling campaigner.

The Helmets for Cyclists Debate is a topic of increasing interest for the **popular press**. It's been calculated that some 150–200 lives a year could be saved if all cyclists wore helmets. By this same logic, if all the people who ride in cars were made to wear helmets, perhaps 3,000–4,000 lives a year would be saved!

Abstract ideas and arguments about helmets create false issues and miss the point. Wearing or not wearing a helmet is an utterly personal decision, and there is really only one fact you need to know. In most fatal and serious bicycle accidents the critical injury is to the head. Even a drop of two feet onto a hard surface is enough to fracture the skull. Wear a helmet whenever you cycle. It's inconvenient. So is not being able to think or talk because your head has been pounded into jelly.

Source: Richard Ballantine, *Richard's New Bicycle Book,* Pan Books, 1990.

a) How does Richard Ballantine use data in the first paragraph? Does the data support his argument?

b) How does he compare 'Abstract ideas' and 'one fact' in the second paragraph?

c) What evidence does he use to support his argument?

d) What is the effect of using an **imperative** for his conclusion?

e) How does he use **emotive language** to confirm his point?

Vocabulary

popular press: material written for the general readership of a population

abstract: theoretical without practical application

🔑 Key terms

imperative: a command or instruction

emotive language: language that appeals to a reader's emotions

4 This extract is from an online scientific research paper.
Make some notes guided by these questions:

a) What conclusion does the article draw about the effects of the compulsory helmet law?

b) Did the law make more cyclists wear helmets?

c) What effect did the law have on child cyclists?

d) What other factors could have caused a decline in head injuries?

e) How does this article use data?

f) What is the effect of the article's references to other studies?

g) Are there any points where this article and Richard Ballantine agree?

> **Vocabulary**
>
> **mandatory**: compulsory; required by law

The first year of the **mandatory** bicycle helmet laws in Australia saw increased helmet wearing from 31 per cent to 75 per cent of cyclists in Victoria and from 31 per cent of children and 26 per cent of adults in New South Wales (NSW) to 76 per cent and 85 per cent. However, the two major surveys using matched before and after samples in Melbourne (Finch et al. 1993; Report No. 45, Monash Univ. Accident Research Centre) and throughout NSW (Smith and Milthorpe 1993; Roads and Traffic Authority) observed reductions in numbers of child cyclists 15 and 2.2 times greater than the increase in numbers of children wearing helmets. This suggests the greatest effect of the helmet law was not to encourage cyclists to wear helmets, but to discourage cycling. In contrast, despite increases to at least 75 per cent helmet wearing, the proportion of head injuries in cyclists admitted or treated at hospital declined by an average of only 13 per cent. The percentage of cyclists with head injuries after collisions with motor vehicles in Victoria declined by more, but the proportion of head injured pedestrians also declined; the two followed a very similar trend. These trends may have been caused by major road safety initiatives introduced at the same time as the helmet law and directed at both speeding and drink-driving.

Source: D. L. Robinson, 'Head injuries and bicycle helmet laws', *Science Direct*, Elsevier, published online 26 February 1999.

5 Both extracts communicate effectively, though in different ways.

a) Who is the target audience for each piece?

b) For what purpose has each been written?

c) How do your answers to these two questions determine the credibility of each source?

Final task

6 Write an evaluation of these two pieces about cycle helmets. You will need to consider:

- the structure of each text

- their use of evidence

- their credibility.

You should aim to write 250–300 words.

? REFLECTION POINT

After reading the evidence, do you think safety measures are purely a matter of individual choice? Should they be made compulsory, or strongly encouraged? Why might people not want to wear a helmet when cycling?

Evaluating and referencing sources and evidence

Skills focus
✓ Evaluation
✓ Communication

Learning focus
- Evaluate sources, considering the author and purpose, recognising that some sources may be more credible than others.
- Discuss the effectiveness of an argument, making explicit reference to its structure and use of evidence.

Big question: How do you know which reference sources you can rely on?

Getting started

When you review evidence to reach a conclusion or make a recommendation, you need to acknowledge where the evidence has come from.

1
a) Working on your own, list all the reference sources used in this chapter so far.

b) Add to your list any sources that you have found yourself.

c) Discuss the sources in your group and tick the ones you feel are particularly important or persuasive.

d) Compare your findings with other groups and explain your decisions.

Exploring

To evaluate a source, you need to think about the purpose and audience – who is the document written for and why?

2 Drawing on your list of sources from question 1, create your own table like this one:

Source	Audience	Purpose
Better Health Channel	General public	To encourage people to walk
Cycling Weekly online magazine	Cycling enthusiasts	To reassure cyclists that cycling is good for them

You will now look more closely at the *Cycling Weekly* article from Unit 4.1, 'Why cycling is great for your legs, lungs, immune system and mind'. In the original article, the writer supported their claim that cyclists enjoy better lung health by citing this source of the information:

Source: *Cycling Weekly* online magazine, 16 August 2022.

'A study by the Healthy Air Campaign, Kings College London, and Camden Council, saw air pollution detectors fitted to a driver, a bus user, a pedestrian and a cyclist using a busy route through central London. The results showed that the driver experienced five times higher pollution levels than the cyclist, as well as three and a half more than the walker and two and a half times more than the bus user. Long story short: the cyclist won.'

The text included a link to an article about the scientific study (shown underlined in the extract above).

3 In your group, discuss these questions and make some notes:

a) Why does the article refer to the Healthy Air Campaign study?

b) How does the reference to the study support *Cycling Weekly*'s point?

c) What are the effects of how the writer uses language to present the research? For example, why list all the groups involved in the study? What is the impact of the final sentence?

d) How effective would the article be without reference to the study?

In discussing these questions, you will probably have made the point that the *Cycling Weekly* article shows **bias**. The online magazine is aimed at a specific group of people who enjoy cycling, as you saw in the table above. *Cycling Weekly* has a **vested interest**, as it will want to encourage bicycle riders that their activity is beneficial to their health. By referring to a **credible** scientific study, *Cycling Weekly* suggests that its message is supported by reputable scientists.

The Healthy Air Campaign study, conducted with a major university and a local authority, is scientific, reaching its conclusions from evidence. It is, therefore, **unbiased**, which makes it a credible source.

> ### 🔑 Key term
>
> **bias**: an inbuilt prejudice
>
> **unbiased**: lacking prejudice, fair
>
> **vested interest**: a personal reason or stake in something, especially expecting financial or some other gain
>
> **credible**: believable or trustworthy

You can watch a video about the Healthy Air Campaign study online; use the search terms 'Healthy Air Campaign, King's College London and Camden council' to access.

4 Now, read the extract from a scientific report from Cambridge University on the next page. Make your own notes on these questions:

a) What is the key conclusion of the paragraph?

b) Is the data about the number of early deaths credible?

c) Why are the Royal Colleges of Physicians and of Paediatrics and Child Health named in full?

Air pollution is one of the leading environmental risk factors for people's health. A recent report from the Royal Colleges of Physicians and of Paediatrics and Child Health suggested that it contributes to around 40 000 early deaths a year in the UK. One of the main sources of air pollution in cities is transport and a shift from cars, motorbikes and buses to active travel would help to reduce emissions. However, people who walk or cycle in such environments will inhale more pollution, which could be detrimental to their health.

Source: 'Walking and cycling good for health even in cities with higher levels of air pollution', University of Cambridge, published online 5 May 2016.

You can see that the reference to a specific scientific report from a reputable body, with **verifiable** data, makes the article's conclusions very persuasive.

> 🔑 **Key term**
>
> **verifiable**: able to be checked as accurate or true

Developing

5 Look at the data in the infographic below.

Global CO$_2$ emissions from transport

Our World in Data

This is based on global transport emissions in 2018, which totalled 8 billion tonnes CO$_2$. Transport accounts for 24% of CO$_2$ emissions from energy.

74.5% of transport emissions come from road vehicles

Road (passenger)	Road (freight)	Aviation	Shipping
(includes cars, motorcycles, buses, and taxis)	(includes trucks and lorries)	(81% passenger; 19% from freight)	10.6%
45.1%	29.4%	11.6%	

Of passenger emissions: 60% from international; 40% from domestic flights

Rail 1%

Other (mainly transport of oil, gas, water, steam and other materials via pipelines) 2.2%

OurWorldinData.org – Research and data to make progress against the world's largest problems.
Data Source: Our World in Data based on International Energy Agency (IEA) and the International Council on Clean Transportation (ICCT). Licensed under CC-BY by the author Hannah Ritchie.

Now, read this sample answer which is based on the infographic and the information in the previous sections:

Source: 'Our World in Data'/International Energy Agency (IEA) and the International Council on Clean Transportation (ICCT).

> A lot of transport emissions come from private cars and these could be reduced if more people walked or used bicycles. Children would also gain a lot of health benefits from walking or cycling to school. In places where the authorities have made particular provision for walking and cycling, there has been a real increase in the numbers of children making their own way to school, on foot or on a bike, rather than relying on their parents' cars.

a) Working with a partner, highlight each factual statement the sample answer makes; for example, the first one is 'A lot of transport emissions come from private cars'. List these in a table.

b) For each factual statement, identify which sources the writer has drawn on.

As you saw with the *Cycling Weekly* article, it is good practice to refer to your sources. This adds credibility to your writing and allows readers to check the information if they are interested. Failing to acknowledge your sources could be seen as **plagiarism**, which would discredit your writing.

To acknowledge the source of the information, the first sentence in the sample answer could be rewritten like this:

> Data from ourworldindata.org shows that a lot of transport emissions come from private cars (https://ourworldindata.org/co2-emissions-from-transport). These could be reduced if more people walked or used bicycles.

An alternative would be to use **footnotes**, in which case the sentence may be written like this:

> Data from the 'Our World in Data' website shows that a lot of transport emissions come from private cars[1]. These could be reduced if more people walked or used bicycles.
>
> [1] https://ourworldindata.org/co2-emissions-from-transport

🔑 Key terms

plagiarism: using someone else's work as if it were your own

footnotes: a method of referencing sources where the details appear at the foot of the page

Language support

Useful phrases to introduce sources:

'Data/Evidence from…'

'According to/As reported by…'

'A study by X showed that…'

'For example, according to…'

'While data from X suggests…, data from Y indicates that…'

Whichever method you choose when referencing sources, you must be consistent throughout your report. The sources you have looked at are from the internet. To acknowledge a book or magazine, you use the author's name, the title, the publisher and the date when the piece was published – for example: Witts, J. *The Bike Book*, Haynes, 2017.

6 On your own, rewrite the rest of the sample answer, adding acknowledgement of the sources used. You can use either method of referencing – remember to be consistent.

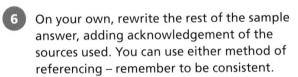

Final task

7 Working in a small group, discuss which sources you think provide the most persuasive information that walking and cycling give health benefits? Then on your own, write a paragraph reviewing the evidence that there are health benefits to cyclists and walkers, using and acknowledging different sources.

- You can use sources you have found in your own research as well as sources in this chapter.
- Try to use the phrases suggested in the Language support box.

❓ REFLECTION POINT

Is there a difference between expressing ideas and judgements that have been influenced by what you have read or seen, and plagiarising – suggesting the ideas are entirely your own? Where do you draw the line? When do you think it is most important to acknowledge that you are leaning on someone else's research, work or ideas?

Proposing a course of action

Skills focus
✓ Analysis
Learning focus
- Recommend an appropriate course of action.
- Explain its application and consequences.

Big question: How do you persuade people to take action?

Getting started

1 Look again at the sources you have read in this chapter and the research you have done. Are there any examples that changed your mind, or that you found particularly persuasive? Which elements had the most effect? For example:

- Was it new evidence you had not considered before, or the way the evidence was communicated?

- Was it particularly persuasive language? Did it clarify causes and consequences effectively?

- Was it a particularly credible source?

Make notes of your responses, then discuss with a partner. Be prepared to share your responses with the class.

Exploring

Read this information from Living Streets, a charity that promotes everyday walking. This is part of a document the charity produced to promote walking to school.

Source: Living Streets.

Why walk to school?

As the UK charity for everyday walking, we have promoted the importance of walking to school for over twenty years. During normal times, the walk to school is the single most accessible way to reduce congestion and pollution outside the school gates, while increasing the safety and improving physical and mental wellbeing of pupils.

A generation ago, 70% of us walked to school – now it's less than half.

We want to reverse this decline. We want children to be energised and empowered, and to make walking to school their natural choice.

Why the Walk to School matters

Happier children

It's been proven that children who do some form of exercise, especially a walk before school, do better in class because they arrive refreshed, fit and ready to learn.

Less congestion

During morning peak traffic times, one in five cars on the road are taking children to school, contributing to congestion, air pollution and carbon emissions.

Cleaner air

The school run alone is responsible for generating half a million tonnes of CO_2 per year (which is more than some small countries!). Imagine what we could achieve if we began converting some of these rides to strides?

2. Make notes in response to the following questions on the Living Streets article, bearing in mind what you have learned in earlier lessons.

   a) How does the article use language to persuade the reader? Think about structure as well as the words used.

   b) What evidence does the article draw on to support its recommendations?

   c) What are the key reasons for the charity's support of walking to school? Are there any reasons you have not considered before? Discuss with your group.

   d) Do the students in your group find the piece persuasive? Why/why not?

Developing

3. Read the following extract from a report on the safety of children cycling in China. The recommendation at the end of the paragraph is that the government should be involved in the implementation of safety measures. Look at the ways the writer builds up to the recommendation.

> Techniques writers use to persuade readers include:
> - structured reasoning
> - use of evidence
> - examples and experience
> - persuasive techniques
> - emotive language.

One of the main strategies used to prevent bicycle-related injuries is the promotion of helmet use, which can reduce the severity of bicycle-related injuries. However, due to economic restrictions, many families in rural China cannot afford to buy these helmets. Another strategy of preventing bicycle-related injuries is environmental modification. A recent systematic review reported that purpose-built bicycle-specific lanes reduced crashes and injuries among cyclists. Unlike urban environments, rural regions commonly have dirt roads and cement roads due to the backward economy and other factors, and motor vehicles, bicycles, and pedestrians share the available lanes. Pedestrian crossings are rare, and there are neither barrier-protected cycle tracks nor bike-designated crossing areas in rural China. Implementation of these preventive measures requires the participation of the government.

1. Cycle helmets are the most helpful safety measure.

2. However, many families cannot afford them.

3. Therefore, the environment needs to be modified.

4. Bike lanes are the most successful.

5. Bike lanes are difficult to implement on rural roads.

6. Government action is therefore recommended.

Source: Yanhu Ji et al, 'An Intervention to Reduce Bicycle Injuries among Middle School Students in Rural China', *International Journal of Environmental Research and Public Health*, published online 26 June 2017.

As this is a formal report, no emotive language is used. Instead, the report uses evidence and clear examples to structure a reasoned support for the recommendation.

a) You have seen that the structure is logical. Do you find it persuasive?

b) Can you find any flaws in the argument?

c) Why might it not be easy for government to act on the proposal?

The Chinese report is making a recommendation to government; the next example puts a proposal to parents. KidsWalk-to-School is a programme run by the US Department of Health and Human Services, which helps parents organise safe walking routes to school for their children. Read the following extract from its booklet:

3. Planning the program on a larger scale

You may want to plan a KidsWalk-to-School program for an entire subdivision, school, or school system. Many of the steps for organizing a larger scale program are similar to the neighborhood program, but there are several considerations:

- Present the program to your school's **PTA**.
- Once you have established interest, form a committee that includes representatives from all participating groups, such as teachers, **crossing guards**, the school principal, and the transportation committee.
- Include all students in the KidsWalk-to-School program and not just the ones who live within walking distance of the school. Everyone can gain from the message of KidsWalk-to-School and participate in different ways. Use some of the other ideas from Program Variations (see p.21): have schoolwide contests for walking the most in a particular week or month or include pedestrian safety, air pollution reduction, physical activity, and related topics in the school curriculum.
- Have each neighborhood come up with a name for their group that distinguishes them from other walk-to-school groups. Design signs for each group that will help young children identify their group at the end of the school day.

4 Work with a partner to discuss the following questions and note down your responses:

Source: 'KidsWalk-to-School; a guide to promote walking to school', National Center for Chronic Disease Prevention and Health Promotion (U.S.), Division of Nutrition and Physical Activity, 2000.

a) What stages of action does the booklet propose? How clear are the recommendations?

b) Identify the use of imperatives.

- How do they match the stages of action?
- Are any proposals made without imperatives? How?
- Are recommendations with and without imperatives equally effective? Why are both used?

c) How are the proposals for action supported? Are the supports helpful and/or persuasive?

> ## Vocabulary
>
> **PTA**: Parent–Teacher Association
>
> **crossing guards**: adults positioned at road crossings to supervise children when crossing the road
>
> **bolster**: support

Final task

The Safe Routes to School National Partnership points out that any programme needs to be inclusive and benefit students with disabilities. It says:

> Students with disabilities are a key group to include when developing and implementing a Safe Routes to School program. On average, one out of every seven students has some type of disability. Students with disabilities can benefit greatly from Safe Routes to School programs, which provide invaluable tools that support healthy lifestyles, **bolster** physical activity, and promote independence. Developing a program that is welcoming for students with disabilities broadens a program's reach, ensures all students can receive the benefits of the program, and enables students with and without disabilities to enjoy each other's company and learn safe and healthy habits together.

Source: Safe Routes to School National Partnership.

5 Working on your own, write three paragraphs proposing actions that would help children with disabilities to take part in a walking and cycling to school strategy. You will need to:

- draw on what you have learned about the issue of cycling and walking to school throughout the chapter

- carry out research as necessary, to support your proposal

- use persuasive language techniques and structures.

Your three paragraphs should include:

a) background: why it is important to include children with disabilities

b) the key benefits that all children would gain

c) a proposal for cycling (adapted bikes, for example)

d) a proposal for walking (accessible routes for wheelchairs, for example).

6 Present your key recommendations to your class in a short speech. The content of each of your paragraphs should be no more than one minute long. Therefore, you will need to note down the key points of each paragraph on a piece of paper or card to use as prompts.

7 Peer-review each other's speeches using the criteria in the 'Checklist for success'.

❷ REFLECTION POINT

Is oral or written communication more effective? Does it change according to speaker/writer and audience? Are particular areas better suited to one form of communication or the other?

Checklist for success

Speech content:
- ✔ Proposal is practical and well supported.
- ✔ Ideas are clearly expressed and organised.
- ✔ Uses persuasive language and techniques.

Delivery:
- ✔ Speaks clearly.
- ✔ Engages audience using tone of voice, eye contact and gestures.

Applying what you have learned

Skills focus
✓ Analysis
✓ Communication
Learning focus
- Identify patterns and trends in graphical or numerical data to support an argument.
- Identify perspectives and synthesise arguments when recommending an appropriate course of action.
- Present coherent, well-reasoned and clearly structured arguments.

Your task

You started this chapter by looking at a study by the World Health Organization (WHO), which showed that globally children's health is suffering because of a lack of physical exercise. You have also looked at several examples of organisations around the world encouraging children to walk or cycle to school to address this problem.

World Health Action is launching a competition for young people who want to make a difference. Here is their competition announcement:

World Health Action

Children's lack of exercise is a global problem – on average, around 80 per cent of young people do not do enough physical exercise.

The results are both physical and mental health problems for children and teenagers.

It is a worldwide problem – but also a local one. What can you do, in your area, to help?

We want you to suggest a scheme for your local area that will encourage young people to be more active. The scheme should be evidence-based and practicable.

Your entry to the World Health Action competition will be a written proposal for a walking and cycling strategy for your school, which uses the evidence you have looked at to support your ideas. You will produce your proposal in a group, and present an oral summary.

Approaching the task

On the next page is a sample plan for a proposal that after-school sports clubs should be made readily available.

| Creating more provision for after-school sports clubs and encouraging students to attend ||
Stage	Evidence/Considerations
Outline of need for more activity	WHO report; Active Health; school survey
Reasons local children don't do more exercise	Online research; local survey; individual stories
Discussion of preferred physical exercise (sport)	School survey; data from local sports clubs
Discussion of barriers to attending sport clubs	School survey; data from local sports clubs; travel times and distances data
Proposal for after-school clubs	Which sports? Who will run them? How will students travel home?
Conclusion	Quick recap of main evidence to support proposal

1 Discuss the plan with a partner.

   a) Does the plan create a logical structure for the proposal?

   b) Does it include appropriate primary and secondary evidence?

   c) Does the plan consider any problems with the proposal?

   d) Can you think of any way the plan might be improved?

Your competition entry proposal will explain how a strategy for your school to encourage more students to walk or cycle to school would work. You will need to take account of the constraints and opportunities of your local area.

Your target audience will be your school's leadership group, so the proposal will need to be very clear and written in a formal style. It will need a clear structure and to use evidence to support your ideas. You should be aiming for about a minimum of 1000 words for the written proposal, and a summary of about 5 minutes for the oral presentation.

Stage 1: Reviewing your learning

2 Look back through your work in this chapter. Take careful note of the skills you have practised and any research or evidence that will be useful for this task. In the table on the right, there is a reminder of some of the important skills you will be able to use.

3 Now make a similar list of the research you have done, both in the chapter and that you have found for yourself from the internet or your own surveys. Use the 'Planning your proposal' section below to select relevant areas of research for each stage.

Consider whether there is any further research you need to do.

Section	Skills
4.1	Summary, citing research data and presenting survey results
4.2	Using reasons to support explanations
4.3	Evaluation of different arguments
4.4	Structuring argument and using evidence
4.5	Making a well-supported proposal for action

4 Finally, remind yourself of language and presentation techniques you have studied in this chapter, including various ways of presenting data and research results.

Stage 2: Planning your proposal

5 **a)** In your group, make some initial notes for the different sections of the proposal. Use the 'Checklist for success' to help you write your proposal.

b) From your notes, make a detailed plan (based on the sample plan above) which shows the stages of your proposal and the evidence you are going to use.

Checklist for success

✔ Show your understanding of the global factors behind the competition – the causes and consequences of:

  ✔ children's health

  ✔ climate and pollution

  ✔ transport issues.

✔ Show the causes and consequences of children's inactivity.

✔ Show your understanding of the relationship between the global concern and your own country and area.

✔ Draw on research to show how increasing walking and cycling to your school could make a difference.

✔ Use a range of sources to support your proposal, including evaluation of both primary and secondary research.

✔ Include evidence and reasoning to support your plan.

✔ Decide on the details of your proposal for this local action in response to the global issue.

✔ Identify what objections or barriers there might be and how these can be overcome.

---

6 Here are three extracts from the after-school sports clubs proposal.

a) Can you match them to these appropriate points in the sample plan?

- Ensuring wide participation

- Gaining suitable volunteers to supervise activities

- The availability of space and equipment.

b) Identify the strengths and weaknesses in these extracts. How could they be improved upon?

> Our survey showed that the most popular sports for participation are rugby, cricket and football, though smaller numbers of students prefer basketball, swimming and squash. Our proposal therefore focuses on the provision of activities, training and matches in rugby, cricket and football. As these are all team sports, they are reliant on numbers of participants, which makes them ideally suited to after-school clubs...

The figures from the WHO study were not completely replicated in our own school survey, but the results were still a matter of concern, as can be seen from the graph…

We recognise that the implementation of our proposal will not be easy. There are several barriers which need to be addressed, such as…

Stage 3: Organising the work

7 Divide up the key tasks among the members of your group. In this way, everyone will make an important contribution.

Some of the areas of responsibility might be:

- choosing and bringing together the key sources
- creating charts, graphs, maps and other illustrations
- writing different sections of the text of the proposal
- organising the final presentation of the proposal document.

Stage 4: Presenting the proposal

8 When presenting your proposal, it is a good idea to:

- Show the organisation with titled sections and list these in a Contents page at the beginning.
- Make sure you have a clear integration of your text, charts and diagrams.
- Proofread your work together very carefully before you hand it in.
- Choose the key points for your 5-minute summary presentation.

9 The class can judge the presentations and choose a shortlist of three for your school's entry into the World Health Action competition. Refer to the 'Checklist for success' at the end of Unit 4.5 to evaluate the presentations.

10 Put all the written proposals out on display and look through all the work produced by the class. Evaluate the effectiveness of each proposal using the 'Checklist for success'.

Checklist for success

✔ The proposal is presented attractively and is well organised.

✔ Data and graphics are used effectively.

✔ The key proposal is practical and persuasive.

Reflecting on your progress

How effectively did your group communicate your ideas? Did you make a full and valuable contribution to the project?

Reflect on what is the most important thing you have learned from this unit.

Giving a personal response

Skills focus
✓ Reflection
Learning focus
- Explain how personal perspective on an issue has changed.
- Identify skills learned or improved during an activity and consider strategies for further development.

Big question: What role does government have over individual decisions?

Getting started

1 With a partner, discuss how you travel to and from school and what influences your choice of transport. For example, you might think about who you travel with, how far you travel and the local environment.

Create a mind map or word diagram to record your ideas.

In earlier units, you saw how different schemes helped to change people's behaviour, encouraging more children to make their own way to school, where possible, and to enjoy the social and health benefits of doing so.

2 **a)** Have any of the resources in this chapter changed the way you think about exercise or travel to school?

b) Have any of the resources in this chapter changed the way you exercise or travel to school?

c) Which research or resources did you find the most influential, and why?

Discuss your responses with a partner.

Exploring

When writing, we communicate the process of change using words and phrases that indicate the sequence and connections. In a flow diagram, the process might be presented like the flow diagram to the right.

Research evidence/data

Changed perspective

Action taken

For example, here are two different experiences:

Sample answer 1:

> Having seen how much walking to school could improve my fitness, I realised that this was something I ought to try. I have therefore decided to walk to school at least three times a week.

Sample answer 2:

> I already cycle to school each day, but now will try to find a less busy route. I understood how my previous route on the main roads was exposing me to pollution after reading research that showed the extent of vehicle emissions.

key

Identifies the research as the cause of change

Acknowledges the change of personal perspective

Identifies the personal action taken

3 Write a short paragraph explaining your own experience, using the flow diagram and the sample answers as models.

In Unit 4.5, you looked at some examples of community action. This extract from the KidsWalk-to-School booklet discusses one of the participants, Max, and shows how his community's changed perspectives has led to several changes in his local area.

4 Read the extract. Working on your own, list:

a) the changes that the KidsWalk-to-School programme has made to the school and the local area

b) who has benefited from the changes.

Vocabulary

sidewalk: path for people to walk alongside a road used by traffic

intersection: point where two or more roads meet

pedestrian: person travelling on foot (walking) rather than by vehicle

forego: go without something

[Max's] community has less traffic, especially around the school, which means there's less pollution and less chance of being hit by a car. Max's parents have become aware of some things in their neighborhood that need improvement and they can bring up these issues at the next town meeting. In addition, crime has gone down in the neighborhood because of the increased presence of adults each day…

The KidsWalk-to-School program has affected Max's neighborhood—the **sidewalks** have been resurfaced and a crossing guard now works at the busy Front Street **intersection** to safely direct **pedestrian** traffic. Because of the success of the KidsWalk-to-School program, during a recent budget debate parents voted to **forego** school bus service in their neighborhood. The money saved with one less bus to maintain and run helps pay for school physical education programs that otherwise would have been cut.

Source: 'KidsWalk-to-School; a guide to promote walking to school', National Center for Chronic Disease Prevention and Health Promotion (U.S.), Division of Nutrition and Physical Activity, 2000.

Developing

You have seen that individual people can make choices for their own lives that will increase their activity levels to benefit their health. You have also seen how local and national governments have encouraged children to be more active and have supported schemes to encourage them to be so.

5 Read the following extract from an article about children walking to school in Malaysia. Discuss and note down your responses to the following questions:

a) What challenges do the children of Kampung Tiku face on their journey to school?

b) What might local or national government do to help them with these challenges?

c) Why do you think that such actions have not already been implemented?

A trek through forest to reach school

by Carolyn Hong, 9 February 2015

The **suspension bridge** high over the rushing Papar River sways and rocks alarmingly but to the children of the jungle school, it is as stable as a paved road in the city.

They run across, stopping to lean over to see the river, tease each other and race on to class. The bridge is part of their daily route to school through the rainforest in Malaysia's Sabah state.

About 20 children, aged six to 12, from Kampung Tiku walk an hour each day to get to school in the neighbouring village of Buayan, and make the return journey home. The trek to school is a reality of life in isolated villages in the vast **interior** of Sabah and Sarawak states on Borneo island where there are limited roads, schools and hospitals.

They start walking at 6 a.m., and often go barefoot but **don** shoes as soon as they reach school, or risk the **wrath** of their teachers.

Their lives seem simpler than those of people in the city and closer to nature. Yet as they grow older, they have to face a different path, one that can be far more challenging. To complete their education, they have to move to towns and cities to attend secondary school, a **wrenching** change for them and their parents. A lack of secondary schools in remote areas means they have little choice.

Source: *The Straits Times.*

Government has a responsibility to provide the population with basic health services and infrastructure but may be limited by the environment and finances available. The families of Kampung Tiku have made individual decisions to overcome the challenges of their environment and the children walk a difficult journey to school. However, some people would argue that most decisions should be made by individuals and that governments should be less involved.

A study by Vanderbilt University in the USA asked people across North and South America to what extent they thought government should ensure the well-being of its citizens. The results of the survey are shown in Figure 4.7.1.

Figure 4.7.1: Average support for government ensuring well-being of the people in the Americas.

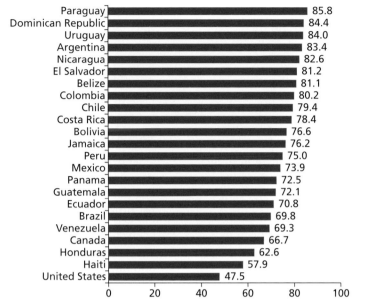

Government responsible for ensuring the well-being of the people (percentage)

Paraguay	85.8
Dominican Republic	84.4
Uruguay	84.0
Argentina	83.4
Nicaragua	82.6
El Salvador	81.2
Belize	81.1
Colombia	80.2
Chile	79.4
Costa Rica	78.4
Bolivia	76.6
Jamaica	76.2
Peru	75.0
Mexico	73.9
Panama	72.5
Guatemala	72.1
Ecuador	70.8
Brazil	69.8
Venezuela	69.3
Canada	66.7
Honduras	62.6
Haiti	57.9
United States	47.5

Source: Margarita Corral, 'To what extent should government ensure citizen well-being', © 2009, Latin American Public Opinion Project, *AmericasBarometer Insights* series.

6 Study Figure 4.7.1 and discuss these questions with a partner:

a) Overall, how strong is the support for government ensuring the well-being of citizens?

b) Can you think of reasons why the USA is at the bottom of the chart?

c) If it is not listed, where do you think your own country would fit into the chart?

d) Where would you place yourself? Why?

Final task

Having reviewed your personal actions and the implementation of various schemes around the world to encourage more students to walk and cycle to school, what is your view? In the last section of this chapter, you contributed to a proposal for a walking and cycling strategy for your school – but is this something you really believe in?

7 Write approximately 200 words communicating your own perspective on how far you think local authorities and governments should invest in incentives for children to walk or cycle to school. To what extent do you think the decision is an individual one for the children and their families?

Use evidence from anywhere in the chapter and follow a similar structure to the flow diagram in the 'Exploring' section earlier.

? REFLECTION POINT

What are the biggest factors that influence your personal decisions? Think about local conditions, but also the expectations of society, your family, your teachers and your friends. Rate each influence on a scale from 1–5 based on how influential it is.

Check your progress

Beginning	Developing	Going beyond
• I can recognise the benefits and challenges of young people taking more exercise.	• I can recognise different perspectives on the benefits and challenges of young people taking more exercise.	• I can evaluate different perspectives about young people taking more exercise and structure an argument about the issue.
• I can make reference to relevant evidence and data.	• I can interpret relevant evidence and data.	• I can explain how relevant evidence and data supports an argument.
• I can recognise the relationship between the causes and consequences of the issues.	• I can discuss the causes of the issues locally and their consequences for others.	• I can evaluate the causes of the issues locally and their consequences for others.
• I can present my ideas and see how they have changed.	• I can show how my ideas have developed and have been influenced by new information.	• I can consider how my ideas have developed and have been influenced by new information gained from research I have undertaken.

Next steps

- Talk to people you know outside school about their perspectives on young people's health and recreational activity. What other measures can be taken to encourage children to have a healthy lifestyle?

- Do you face any barriers to participation in health and recreational activities? What about other people in your local community? How might these barriers be overcome? Carry out research to support your understanding of this issue. What recommendations would you make to help people overcome the barriers to participation you have identified?

- Consider whether your own views have changed while working on this chapter. Do you have a different attitude to walking, cycling or participating in sports?

Planning and writing your research report

Preparing for assessment

5

In this chapter, you will be exploring how to conclude your Stage 9 studies with a piece of research. Instead of developing your thoughts about a particular topic, you will choose a topic for yourself. You will then produce an extended piece of written work that will help your teachers assess your progress as a student of Cambridge Lower Secondary Global Perspectives.

In this chapter, you will be following a step-by-step process to understand how to create a research report. In the process, you will learn from the example of two fictional students, Ayesha and Kito. The examples of their work included in the chapter have been written by the authors of this book.

You will consider:

- **how to choose an appropriate issue**
- **where to find a range of sources reflecting global and national perspectives**
- **how to analyse and evaluate different perspectives**
- **how to present primary and secondary research**
- **how to present a realistic course of action.**

You will be reviewing and applying the research, analysis, evaluation, communication and reflection skills you have been developing in Stage 9:

5.1 Exploring a range of relevant research questions and identifying the best one for you

5.2 Identifying a range of different sources to locate relevant information

5.3 Identifying and linking different perspectives, exploring causes and consequences

5.4 Selecting research methods to answer your question

5.5 Organising your findings and planning your research writing

5.6 Writing up your report with an introductory analysis of the issue

5.7 Developing your argument by evaluating different perspectives

5.8 Making a recommendation for action

5.9 Proofreading, checking and referencing your final report

5.10 Providing a critical bibliography

5.11 Explaining how your personal perspective has changed as a result of research

5.12 Reflecting on skills development and targets for improvement.

Your final task will be to present the finished version of your research report, with a concluding reflection, bibliography and brief evaluation of the sources used.

Exploring a range of relevant research questions and identifying the best one for you

Skills focus
✓ Research
Learning focus
- Formulate a range of relevant questions.
- Identify the best research question to follow up for your research report.

Big question: What makes a relevant research topic?

Getting started

An individual research topic needs to be your own choice and personal to you. However, your teacher will ask you to form groups by topic and may choose which group you go into.

You can work out a suitable issue for research by reviewing the different Global Perspectives topics. Most of these have been explored through a chapter in the Student's Books for Stages 7 to 9, and others have been referenced in those chapters.

1 Working on your own, review the list of Global Perspectives topics below. Which have you studied in depth in your lessons? Which are less familiar to you?

Arts in society	Employment	Poverty and inequality
Change in culture and communities	Environment, pollution and conservation	Social identity and inclusion
Climate change, energy and resources	Globalisation	Sport and recreation
	Health and wellbeing	Technology, industry and innovation
Conflict and peace	Law and criminality	Transport, travel and tourism
Development, trade and aid	Media and communication	Values and beliefs
Digital world	Migration and urbanisation	Water, food and agriculture
Education for all	Political power and action	

Global Perspectives topics are about changes in the world around us and how we prepare for future changes. They raise questions about the causes of change, the consequences at a global and a national level and the actions we can take to deal with those changes.

In your research project, you will need to identify global, national and personal perspectives on the issue you have chosen. You will therefore need to choose:

- a broad topic area from those above
- a specific issue
- a national or local problem that needs a solution.

2 a) Identify the topic that has interested you most on this course and which you feel is an important issue for your own country. On a placard or card, write down the topic and your first thoughts about specific issues you want to explore.

b) Go around the class and find others who have chosen the same broad topic. Form a group around your topic. Together, discuss why this topic raises issues for your country.

Exploring

3 a) Now, on the back of your topic placard, identify and write down a specific issue that is debated in your country today.

b) Then, identify and write down a local, regional or national problem related to this issue – and which needs a solution.

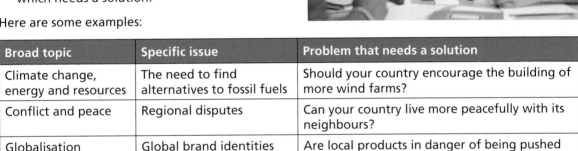

Here are some examples:

Broad topic	Specific issue	Problem that needs a solution
Climate change, energy and resources	The need to find alternatives to fossil fuels	Should your country encourage the building of more wind farms?
Conflict and peace	Regional disputes	Can your country live more peacefully with its neighbours?
Globalisation	Global brand identities	Are local products in danger of being pushed out by global brands?

4 You will now take part in a 'marketplace' exercise.

a) One person from each group stays and becomes the 'teacher'; the teacher's role is to tell members from other groups about your group's topic, issue and problem.

b) The other group members each visit a different class group to learn about the other group's topic, issue and problem.

c) Reform your original group. Share feedback on what you learned. Which questions do people really want answers to?

d) Finally, consider whether anyone wants to change topic and group.

You will be staying in your topic group for the rest of this chapter. Each of you needs to research a different issue and question, but you will be sharing different stages of your planning, drafting and writing with each other.

Evaluating

You are now ready to decide on your own research question. The 'Checklist for success' gives the features of a successful research question.

> ### Checklist for success
> ✔ Explores a broad topic.
> ✔ Analyses a specific issue.
> ✔ Presents different perspectives.
> ✔ Makes links between a global problem and a defined national perspective.
> ✔ Can be answered by a specific action.

Revising what you have learned
Unit 1.1 provides guidance about how to ask appropriate research questions.

5 **a)** Read the examples of student questions below. In your group, discuss and evaluate them. What are their strengths and weaknesses? Place them in rank order. How could the weaker questions be improved?

A. Leeto wants to write about 'Digital World'. Their question is: 'What will be the next big advance in technology?'

B. Mangala has chosen 'Poverty and inequality'. Their question is: 'What are the causes of relative poverty and what actions can address this problem in my country?'

C. Charlie has chosen 'Employment'. Their question is: 'How can our schools prepare students better for future employment?'

D. Kito has chosen 'Water, food and agriculture'. Their question is: 'Do vegetarians eat healthier food?'

E. Helen wants to explore 'Transport, travel and tourism'. Their question is: 'Should petrol and diesel cars be banned from our city centres?'

F. Ayesha wants to study 'Climate change, energy and resources'. Their question is: 'Is global warming the result of human actions?'

b) On paper, agree on a better version of three weaker questions that:

- can be answered with reference to local action

- are more focused

- refer to national issues (either in your home country or other countries you know about)

- present competing perspectives.

c) Share your revised questions with the class. Together, discuss what makes a SMART question.

> **Revising what you have learned**
> ....
> An explanation of SMART targets is provided in the Stage 8 Student's Book, Chapter 1.

Developing

You are going to continue following Ayesha and Kito, students with different strengths. They both enjoy Global Perspectives because of the opportunity to learn about how issues that are important at home are also global problems and how research can help to find solutions for the future.

Following discussion, Ayesha, who attends an international school in Germany, has changed her question to:

'Is climate change responsible for global flooding and what local actions can we take in Germany to conserve resources?'

Kito goes to school in Qatar and has decided he wants to focus on the possible advantages of eating less meat, so he has changed his question to:

> 'What are the possible advantages of a plant-based diet and is this practical in Qatar, which imports much of its food?'

6 **a)** With a partner, discuss whether Ayesha's and Kito's questions meet the targets identified in the checklist.

    b) How did Ayesha and Kito change their questions to achieve this?

You will track the ways in which Ayesha and Kito improve their research, analysis, evaluation and communication skills as they plan and write their projects.

Applying

7 **a)** Now, choose a research question of your own and draft it carefully in pencil on a piece of card. Write in plain English and keep the question as short as you can. It must be a question:

- that is based on a broad topic but focused on a specific issue
- which you can research information about
- which it is possible to have different views on
- which is important for your own country or a country you are familiar with
- that raises a problem to which there is a possible solution
- to which you can give an answer based on research, analysis and evaluation.

    b) Share your draft questions within your group.

    c) Then, move on to another group and ask them if they like your topic and question.

    d) Make changes based on feedback.

> **❓ REFLECTION POINT**
>
> Based on your work in this unit, do you understand what makes a question good to research?
>
> You may need to adapt – or refine – your research question as you find out more about the issue you are researching.
>
> Throughout the process of writing your report, you will be keeping a reflective journal that you can share with your teacher. Write out your question and your thoughts about it.

Identifying a range of different sources to locate relevant information

Skills focus
✓ Research
Learning focus
• Identify and use a wide range of sources to research different perspectives.

Big question: What makes a good range of sources?

Getting started

You have decided on your research topic, your specific issue and your focused question. What next? You will need to do some secondary research and find some perspectives on the issue. Where will you find them?

1 Discuss these questions with a partner. Make notes to feed back to the class.

   a) What are the advantages and disadvantages of simply typing your question into a search engine?

   b) What can you do to ensure that your search is focused and will identify contrasting but credible sources?

Exploring

In your topic groups, you should now each have a specific question that you are going to research. The question may still need refining, but it will have global and national perspectives. As you are researching the same topic area, you will be able to help each other in finding sources, although your final choices of arguments need to be your own.

Good sources should be:

✔ published on credible news websites, academic publications and journals or, for example, government or NGO (non-governmental organisation) websites and blogs

✔ **fact-checked**

✔ **peer-reviewed**

✔ named articles

✔ based on facts

✔ arguments, not assertions.

You will need to find two different global sources and two different national sources from your own country or a country you are familiar with. Check who has published these sources and what interests they represent.

🔑 Key terms

fact-checked: a key element of responsible news media is that any claims and statistics are fact-checked by in-house teams and lawyers to avoid false claims and 'fake news'

peer-reviewed: the peer-review process is important to academic publication, and involves checking the validity of the research and its claims by other academics working in the field before publication

2 Discuss where you could locate those perspectives on your topic with others in your group and draw a spider diagram. It might look like this one. These questions all have international and national perspectives.

Toni: Can we make our diet healthier?

Umair: Can we prepare for future pandemics?

Abim: Can we encourage more healthy exercise?

Our topic: Health and wellbeing
Places to find sources:
- World Health Organization (WHO) website – global
- Harvard Health publishing (Harvard Medical School website) – global
  - Government website
  - National news website

Alvina: Can we provide the essentials for good teenage mental health?

Veer: Can we provide better support for elderly people?

3 **a)** Each person in the topic group can now use the national and international sources to find two global and two national perspectives on their question. Remember: a perspective is an argument based on facts and evidence.

b) Share your discoveries with your group.

4 Now, on a piece of poster paper, create a spider diagram with facts and arguments linked to your overall topic area and based around shared, reliable sources.

Display your poster to the rest of the class.

Evaluating

Ayesha, who attends an international school in Germany, is researching: 'Is climate change responsible for global flooding and what local actions can we take in Germany to conserve resources?' Her spider diagram looks like this:

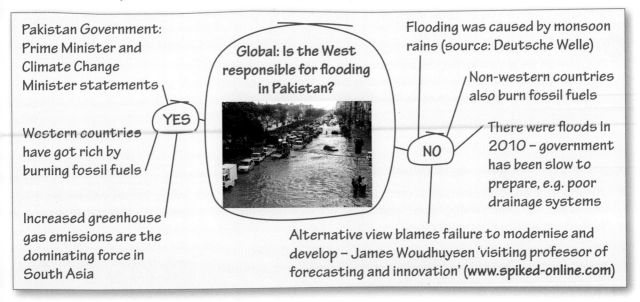

Pakistan Government: Prime Minister and Climate Change Minister statements

Western countries have got rich by burning fossil fuels

Increased greenhouse gas emissions are the dominating force in South Asia

Global: Is the West responsible for flooding in Pakistan?

YES

NO

Flooding was caused by monsoon rains (source: Deutsche Welle)

Non-western countries also burn fossil fuels

There were floods in 2010 – government has been slow to prepare, e.g. poor drainage systems

Alternative view blames failure to modernise and develop – James Woudhuysen 'visiting professor of forecasting and innovation' (www.spiked-online.com)

Ayesha has added another 'spider diagram' to explore national solutions to the issue of flooding caused by climate change:

Since 1990, Germany has reduced its emissions of greenhouse gases by 35.7% (bundesregierung.de)

Phase out coal generation

Wind power is the most important renewable energy resource

Government intends to reduce emissions by 55% by 2030

National solution: What can we do in Germany?

Rethink how we heat our homes and how much we travel

'Germany is one of a handful of countries globally to have enshrined the goal of climate neutrality in law' (Source: **Clean Energy Wire** funded by European Climate Foundation) – this includes greenhouse gases

Meeting targets for 2030 depends on transport sector and heating buildings

5 You have looked at Ayesha's plan (spider diagram). Now help Kito with his planning. His research question is: 'What are the possible advantages of a plant-based diet and is this practical in Qatar, which imports much of its food?'

a) Research some possible arguments and sources for Kito.

b) Complete his spider diagram.

Ayesha and Kito are taking slightly different approaches:

- Ayesha is especially concerned to establish the credibility of claims linking climate change and flooding before moving on to look at national and local solutions.

- Kito needs to establish the credibility of a global claim that plant-based foods are healthier and better for the environment, before applying them to a particular national context.

> **Revising what you have learned**
> ....
> Unit 2.1 gives you detailed guidance about exploring different perspectives on the same issue; Unit 2.3 explores the credibility of different sources.

6 **a)** How does Ayesha's approach address the need for a balanced report that identifies possible bias?

b) Where can she find out more about the impact of national and local actions?

c) The global claims Kito is investigating are perhaps less controversial.

- How will Kito find global perspectives supported by evidence?

- What will be the local consequences of these global claims?

- What will be the specific national perspective on this issue for the country where he goes to school?

- What local or national actions are possible or realistic?

Applying

You may have noticed that Ayesha's two global sources differ in their degree of credibility and possible bias.

7 **a)** Draw a table like the one below of the **global** sources you will be exploring and apply the RAVEN test to evaluate their credibility.

b) Then, repeat this process for the **national** sources you will be using.

		Global source A	Global source B	National source A	National source B
R	**Reputation**: Why is this a respected source?				
A	**Ability to observe**: Has the writer seen evidence?				
V	**Vested interest**: Who does the writer represent and what are their interests?				
E	**Expertise**: How expert are the opinions expressed?				
N	**Neutrality**: Are arguments put forward in a neutral or biased way?				

> ❓ REFLECTION POINT
>
> - Do you have enough sources to explore both the facts about the issue and different arguments about it?
>
> - Have you found specific national perspectives as well as global perspectives on the issue you are exploring?
>
> - Do those sources help you to identify issues in need of action?
>
> - Does your question need more refinement?
>
> Share your reflections with your group and write down your personal progress in your reflective journal.

Identifying and linking different perspectives, exploring causes and consequences

Skills focus

✓ Analysis

Learning focus

- Identify and synthesise different perspectives.
- Make links between causes and consequences.

Big question: How do I identify different perspectives on an issue?

Getting started

A **perspective** is a series of **arguments** based on evidence. Once you have found reliable sources, based on observation and evidence that has been fact-checked, you need to start exploring the different arguments that writers are putting forward.

1 Revisit the global sources you explored in Unit 5.2, as well as any other sources on your topic you have found. Within your group, consider:

a) What claims are the writers making? What reasons and evidence do they use to support those claims?

b) Can you separate the causes and consequences of the issue they are exploring in order to evaluate different stages of their arguments?

> ### 🔑 Key terms
>
> **perspective**: a viewpoint on an issue based on evidence and reasoning
>
> **argument**: a series of statements containing reasons and evidence which support a claim about a global issue

Exploring

Here is an example that Kito has found to support his arguments about plant-based diets. He has annotated his source to analyse claims, causes and consequences:

Biodiversity loss

It's not just forests that are in danger from the meat industry. As land is repurposed to raise animals and grow soybean, many habitats are destroyed or impacted. Many species face extinction or are under threat due to the destruction of natural environments.

Estimates suggest that around half of the planet's habitable land is used for agriculture, with roughly 77% of this used by grazing cattle, sheep, goats and other livestock.

Viewpoint to support global argument

Fact

This is a claim: is it supported by evidence?

Cause

Greenhouse gas emissions

Meat consumption is responsible for releasing greenhouse gases such as methane, CO_2 and nitrous oxide. These gases contribute to climate change, such as global warming. Livestock farming contributes to these greenhouse gases in several ways:

— Consequences

— Reasoning to link causes and consequences

- *The destruction of forest ecosystems.* As mentioned above, this process releases enormous amounts of CO_2 into the atmosphere.
- *Raising livestock.* Animals such as cows and sheep create large amounts of methane as they digest food.

— Supporting evidence

- *Decaying manure.* The manure that **ruminant** animals produce also releases methane.
- *Fertiliser use.* Many fertilisers used in soybean production are nitrogen-based, and these produce nitrous oxide emissions.

— Supporting factual detail: it's not just meat that causes problems

Source: 'Is eating meat bad for the environment?', FutureLearn website, 11 May 2021.

2 Annotate your own sources and discuss your annotations with a partner from your group.

a) Can you clearly separate claims, causes and consequences?

b) Have you found supporting factual evidence and arguments?

> **Vocabulary**
>
> **ruminant:** animals that need to chew their food slowly to digest it

3 You will now use Diamond nine to prioritise nine different arguments you have discovered as global claims about the issue you are researching.

a) Put the most important arguments at the top of the diamond and the least important at the bottom. Present the reasons why you have made these choices to the rest of the group. Be prepared to listen to a challenge from other group members. Could the priority of arguments be different?

b) Kito's Diamond nine on the consequences of large-scale meat production is shown as an example. Do you agree with his priorities?

> Sustainability
>
> Greenhouse gas emissions   Water usage
>
> Loss of biodiversity   Human health   Climate change
>
> Animal welfare   Deforestation
>
> Soil degradation

4 Now consider the arguments from the perspective of your own nation or region.

a) What are the priorities for your own region, nation and locality? As a group, discuss whether this would change the order of each argument in the diamond.

b) Has one argument consistently emerged as the most important one for the issue you are researching? That should be your starting point and should allow you to investigate causes and consequences.

Evaluating

You will now explore the way an argument supports its claims by stating causes and consequences.

5 Take the main argument that has emerged from the Diamond nine activity and break it down into the different parts that make up an argument.

a) Discuss with a partner from your group to show your understanding of causes and consequences. Use the bulleted list to guide your discussion.

- What is the main problem?
- How has it come about?
- How do we know?
- What follows on from those causes?

- How do we know those consequences arise from those causes?
- How might bias influence this argument? Are there vested interests at stake?

b) Copy and complete the table on the right with reference to your own chosen issue.

Claim	
Causes	
Supporting evidence	
Consequences	
Supporting reasoning	
Possible bias	

In the previous unit, we saw how Ayesha looked at how far climate change is responsible for flooding in Pakistan. Her sources, *Deutsche Welle* and the website spiked.com, approached the argument differently: one of them focuses on the politics of claims about the causes of flooding, while the other looks more at the science.

6 **a)** Which source is more useful in establishing causes and consequences?

b) Which source is more useful in establishing different lines of argument and possible bias?

7 Kito has analysed an argument about the possible advantages of a plant-based diet. Using the table above, he has looked at the EAT-Lancet Summary Report published in 2019.

Has Kito put some of his material in the wrong column? Can you correct his table for him? Discuss with a partner.

Revising what you have learned

Unit 2.2 gives you examples of how to define causes and consequences when analysing a source, while Unit 4.2 looks at causes and consequences in relation to global and national sources.

Claim	A diet rich in plant-based food and with fewer animal source foods provides both improved health and environmental benefits.
Causes	Healthy diets have an optimal calorific intake with unsaturated fats and limited amounts of processed foods and added sugars.
Supporting evidence	Red meat is a high protein source but makes a low calorific contribution: there are health risks in unbalanced diets.
Consequences	Transformation to healthy diets will require a doubling in the consumption of fruit, vegetables and nuts and a greater than 50% reduction of added sugars and red meat.
Supporting reasoning	Dietary changes from current diets towards healthy diets could prevent 11 million deaths per year according to three different methods of risk analysis.
Possible bias	37 leading scientists from 16 countries in various disciplines. Bias is towards action based on scientific principles. Clear scientific targets are set for improving human health and environment sustainability.

Applying

It is important to clearly separate the causes of the issue you are researching from its consequences.

8   **a)** Take the main argument you are going to evaluate and write a paragraph explaining the causes of the problem and its global consequences if nothing is done. Make sure your evidence is supported by reasoning.

     b) Now, explain why this argument is global in nature: how does it affect everyone and can you produce evidence from different countries to demonstrate this?

Look at Ayesha's introductory argument:

> Most scientists agree that climate change is responsible for global flooding in 2022 in Pakistan (my chosen country of focus) and in the Ahr valley close to where I go to school in Germany. Some have challenged the extent to which early industrialisation in the Global North has caused extreme weather events in the Global South, especially in countries subject to monsoon flooding. Rina Saeed Khan, a Pakistani journalist specialising in environmental issues, has argued that disaster preparedness could have been better (Shairani & Begg, Deutsche Welle 2022). However, human-produced climate change is a global issue and certainly a consequence of global warming caused by greenhouse gas emissions. Without a change in the way all countries produce their power, extreme weather events are likely to be more frequent.

The argument is developing well, with examples that prove the issue is global, debate about causes and consequences (supported by reference to research) and suggestions about action. There are clear links between the global topic of climate change and the global and national issues to be analysed. The argument is still a little assertive, but more factual evidence and reasoned supporting examples can now be the focus.

     c) Looking again at your sources, which ones will help you to deepen your research into the global issue and different national perspectives on it?

Monsoon rains in Pakistan.

❓ REFLECTION POINT

Add the final version of the Diamond nine activity for your research question in your reflective journal.

- Which arguments will you prioritise (a) globally and (b) nationally?

- Can you break these down into causes and consequences?

Consider how you are going to introduce the issue and its relationship to the global topic, by presenting its causes and consequences.

In your reflective journal, draft a short introductory paragraph to the issue you want to explore. You will return to this later in the chapter.

Selecting research methods to answer your question

Skills focus
✓ Research
Learning focus
• Select suitable methods.
• Put predictions and questions to the test.

• •

Big question: What are the national and local perspectives on this issue?

Getting started

Your research report will cover both global and national perspectives, so you will need a clear and explicit national perspective on the issue you have chosen, based on two or more relevant and detailed examples.

First, you need to choose a country: normally this would be the country you are living in and where you go to school, but you could choose the country you were born in, or where many members of your family live, or a country you are familiar with and that has a strong perspective on the issue. It does need to be a country you know well enough to present a specific and realistic local solution to the global problem you are investigating.

1 Working on your own at first, and then sharing with the group who are investigating the same broad topic as yourself:

   a) Choose your nation and explain why it is personal to you.

   b) Identify the reason why your nation has a perspective on the issue.

   c) Analyse the national arguments about this issue and why it is a particular problem for your country.

   d) List some news and newspaper websites where you will be able to find more facts and information.

   e) What other kinds of sources will help you? Are these English language sources? Can you translate them?

   f) Is there controversy about the issue in your country? What are the arguments for or against action?

Exploring

You will need at least two different national perspectives. There are always arguments for and against a specific course of action, so that should be your starting point.

2 Find and share with your group two different national perspectives on the issue you are investigating. Make sure that each perspective is supported by evidence from your chosen country about why a change in attitudes and action would be beneficial for that country or region or detrimental to it. Each viewpoint needs to be supported by evidence and reasoning.

There will be people arguing against change. They come up with reasons and evidence to anticipate that the action will not work.

Copy and complete a table like the one on the right for each national perspective.

Proposed action	
Reasons for/against	
Supporting facts	
Supporting arguments	
Why this would be beneficial/detrimental for the country	

3 **a)** In pairs, role play the different arguments for and against a proposed action or change which is a likely recommendation of your research by acting out different voices in the debate.

- One of you is in favour of action ('the advocate').

- One of you is against ('the objector').

- Make sure your arguments are supported.

- Speak for at least one minute.

- Then swap roles.

b) Now role play the arguments for and against your partner's recommendation.

c) Have clear national perspectives and attitudes towards change emerged?

Evaluating

To find out for yourself whether a proposed local course of action is likely to succeed, it helps to conduct primary research. In Stages 7 and 8, you learned that questionnaires are a good way to work out effective local solutions to a global problem – they can be used to test whether people agree there is a problem and how far they are prepared to change their behaviour to reach a solution.

4 Construct a questionnaire, poll, survey or set of interview questions on your proposed national or local action, to share with local stakeholders. This will establish whether your proposed action has local support.

Remember that your goals need to be SMART: specific, measurable, achievable, realistic and time bound. Your questionnaire will need to determine whether your proposed solution is achievable by asking questions:

- about attitudes to the issue

- which find out how much support there is for change

- about a specific set of actions

- about how likely or unlikely respondents are to carry out that action.

You can ask two types of question:

- closed questions, requiring yes or no answers

- attitude questions using a sliding scale to measure attitudes to change, such as:

> Very likely   Likely   Neither likely nor unlikely   Unlikely   Very unlikely.

You will need to consider:

✔ the best format for your questionnaire

✔ how you can easily extract data about people's opinions (for example, as percentages).

Remember to use clear language and wording for your questions. Include a small number of very specific questions based around whether people would support specific actions.

Finally, remember to thank participants for their time at the end of the questionnaire.

Sent out as a paper or online questionnaire, these questions will allow you to quickly determine some measurable data about the level of support for your arguments and your proposals.

Applying

5 Working on your own, send your questionnaire to friends, classmates, teachers, neighbours and family, to find out their views about a solution to the problem you are analysing.

Try to ensure you have a balance of ages and possible views (so that your sample is 'representative'). This will enable you to test whether your proposal is a realistic local solution to a global and national problem.

Revising what you have learned

Unit 2.5 gives you examples of how to put together questionnaires or surveys to test the community's likely response to a proposed local action.

Kito has decided that his local action will be through his school community, a defined locality that he can easily and safely survey. His proposal, after interviewing and consulting the school caterers, is to introduce two days of meat-free eating at his school. The chef has suggested six possible menus.

Kito is going to survey students and staff at his school to ask them to choose a menu and will also ask them about their attitudes to meat-free food. The first question will be a closed poll, while the second will survey attitudes. He will ask how likely those surveyed are to choose a meat-free alternative to their normal meal.

After the week with two meat-free days, Kito will provide posters with information about what he is doing and why. He will then survey his stakeholders again: he will repeat the original question about choosing a meat-free alternative, survey attitudes to the meal itself using a rating scale and ask a yes/no question to measure how many would support one or two meat-free days a week.

6 **a)** Why did Kito choose to survey his sample twice?

b) What kind of data will this generate?

c) How will it prove the likely success of his action?

d) What kind of national or local action might Kito propose?

7 Make notes on how you will handle the data you have generated from your survey and how it will support your proposed action.

❓ REFLECTION POINT

In the last four units, you have identified:

- a question

- a global perspective on the issue which has clear causes and consequences

- different national perspectives on possible solutions

- a specific local or national action which has support and is likely to succeed.

In your reflective journal, summarise each of these.

- Are there any problems you have identified with your question or your recommended course of action? This is a good moment to make tweaks and changes.

- Do you have enough facts and information to support global and national perspectives on the issue? You now have time to do some additional research to support.

Organising your findings and planning your research writing

Skills focus

✓ Research

Learning focus

- Organise and record information from your research.
- Justify the method you have chosen.

• •

Big question: What does your research prove?

Getting started

This unit supports you to understand how to plan a research report effectively, in order to write up your research.

1 With a partner, recap the way we analyse and evaluate perspectives:

a) What do we call the reasons why there is a problem?

b) What do we call the issues that then follow?

c) What do we need to evaluate when choosing sources of information?

d) What do we call it when a source is unbalanced and strongly promotes a particular perspective?

e) Why do you need to explore a range of different sources of information?

Exploring

2 Copy and complete the table on page 123 to present your plan to your partner in the group you are working in. The table asks you to set out your topic clearly and identify three arguments, sources or pieces of evidence under each heading.

Completing the table will enable you to list the ingredients of a research report – the precise order in which you put all these elements together will depend on your own choices in response to the materials you are studying. However, doing this will help to give you a clear sense of the issue and its global consequences before exploring other arguments and perspectives.

There is no one model for structuring a research report, so you will be trying out several different planning tools: use the one best for you for your final report.

Broad topic			
Specific issue			
Research question			
Causes			
Consequences			
Why is this a global problem? Give evidence.			
Why is this a national problem? Give two examples.			
Compare and contrast global and national perspectives			
Three different perspectives about national solutions to the issue from different sources (one global, two national)	Global:	National:	National:
Evaluation of source credibility, reliability and bias			
What would be a realistic local solution, who supports it, and how can you be sure it is a SMART solution?			

Evaluating

3 Here is Kito's plan about plant-based diets in Qatar. Read through his plan and compare with your own plan. Is there anything you want to revise?

Broad topic	Water, food and agriculture		
Specific issue	Plant-based diets: are they more sustainable?		
Research question	What are the possible advantages of a plant-based diet and is this practical in Qatar, which imports much of its food?'		
Causes	Half of all farmed animal emissions come from beef and lamb (Poore & Nemecek, 2018).	Meat eating can contribute to heart disease and to bowel cancer (nitrates).	Twice as much water is needed to produce beef than other meats, and four times as much to produce alternative protein sources, e.g. lentils (www. futurelearn.com).
Consequences	Food contributes to 25% of global greenhouse gas emissions, so contributing to climate change.	Changes from current diets towards healthy diets could prevent around 11 million deaths a year.	Livestock production wastes land and water resources, and can contaminate water. A plant-based diet is healthier and more sustainable.

Why is this a global problem? Give evidence.	UN's Intergovernmental Panel on Climate Change	EAT-Lancet Commission on Food, Planet, Health	https://www.futurelearn.com/info/blog/eating-meat-bad-for-environment
Why is this a national problem? Give two examples.	Food is a global concern, but it is a national problem in Qatar, which imports 90% of its food.	Poultry is imported from Saudi Arabia, meat products from Australia, New Zealand and India.	'Qatar is possibly the most water-stressed country on earth' (US World Resources Institute). Qatar's government is increasing reservoir capacity, but in a desert country, water is a scarce resource.
Compare and contrast global and national perspectives	Global: we need to reduce our heavy dependency on processed meat products	National: Qatar has particular issues with food security, as it is largely desert, with a scarce water supply and shortage of arable land; it has national reasons for reducing dependency on meat imports	
Three different perspectives about solutions to the issue from different sources	Global: BBC Future – 'Why the vegan diet is not always green'	National: EcoMENA, 'Food Security Strategy in Qatar'	National: 'Qatar national food security strategy'
Evaluation of credibility, reliability and bias	Fact-checked global source – BBC World Service	Volunteer-driven sustainability platform for Middle East	Report in Qatar Tribune includes interview with Minister of Municipality
What would be a realistic local solution, who supports it, and how can you be sure it is a SMART solution?	Research food sourcing by our school caterer. How far is it sustainable and healthy? Would a meat-free day twice a week be viable?	Primary research: interview caterers about options Questionnaire to students, parents and teachers	This would be specific, measurable and achievable: it would be relevant and effective if it reduced emissions and food miles.

Mangrove trees growing in the Ammunition Reservoir, Qatar.

Applying

4 **a)** Share your plan with a partner and assess each other's plans. Copy and complete the table below to evaluate your partner's work.

Target	Working towards target (✔)	Just achieving target (✔)	Confidently achieving target (✔)
Relevant and focused question			
Effective analysis of causes and consequences			
Clearly explained global and national perspectives supported by evidence and examples			
Global and national perspective compared			
Different sources and arguments evaluated			
A specific, realistic and achievable local action			

b) Share your assessment with your partner and give each other verbal feedback. Use three stars and a wish: identify three things that work well and one that needs improvement.

❓ REFLECTION POINT

This unit should have given you a clear plan for your report.

- Do you understand the structure of your report?

- Are you confident that you can demonstrate understanding of the issue and analyse it in your introductory section?

- Are you able to separate out different perspectives?

- Can you evaluate your sources of information?

- Can you propose realistic solutions?

In your reflective journal, copy and complete this table:

Introduction: the problem	
Analysis of causes and consequences	
Evaluation of global perspectives (a solution?)	
Evaluation of different national perspectives (will the solution work for us?)	
Recommendation (what we can do)	

With a clear outline of the problem and the potential solutions, you are ready to write up, giving evidence and reasoning to support your case.

Writing up your report with an introductory analysis of the issue

Skills focus
✓ Analysis

Learning focus
- Identify and synthesise different perspectives.
- Make links between causes and consequences.

Big question: Why is this an important global issue?

Getting started

The process of writing your research report involves clearly identifying various perspectives on the issue you are investigating, bringing together the arguments and information you have found from different sources.

1 **a)** Review your notes in your reflective journal. Begin with the argument at the top of your Diamond nine. Keep your sources alongside you as you write up what you have discovered about different perspectives.

b) Share your proposed starting point with your topic group.

Approaching the task

In this unit, you will be writing up your report in sections under subheadings. You will draw on the sources you have already researched to introduce the issue by analysing its causes and consequences. You will then evaluate two different global perspectives on what should be done.

Section heading	Content	Word limit
Title	Your question	20 words
Introductory analysis	What is the problem and why is it a global problem?	200 words
Evaluating global perspectives	What should we all be doing about this issue in the future? Give two different perspectives on the issue. Why are they global perspectives? Which is more persuasive and why?	200 words

2 Draft your introductory analysis and then swap with a partner from your topic group and read each other's work. Feed back using the 'Checklist for success'.

Evaluating

3 Remember Ayesha and Kito? They have now written introductory paragraphs. Read them and evaluate their strengths and weaknesses.

Checklist for success

Does the draft introduction:

✔ make the issue clear to a reader who has not done the research

✔ provide supporting factual evidence

✔ explain why the evidence is reliable?

Is climate change responsible for global flooding, and what local actions can we take in Germany to conserve resources?

I decided to research this topic because it was a shocking news item in 2022, which had a personal impact on me. The damage and loss of life were caused by monsoon rainfall between June and August. While flooding has also produced severe problems here in Germany, the Pakistan floods were especially catastrophic. I wanted to establish the extent to which our own actions in the West could have contributed to this disaster and what we could do in the future. First, I wanted to establish that this was a global problem and not just a national one. A Minister in Pakistan said the West was to blame: 'I would not like to be **hectored** by Western nations' (Deutsche Welle 'Fact Check') but climate change sceptics such as Professor James Woudhuysen blamed population growth and 'Pakistan's failure to modernise and develop'. The government may have its own bias, wanting to defend its actions and record by blaming others, but Prof Woudhuysen's argument ignores the scale of climate change, and the history of development in the West.

The cause of the flooding was the dramatic increase in intensity of the monsoon season rainfall in recent years, but 2022 appears to be exceptional and graphical evidence supports this.

However, the increase in extreme weather events has occurred alongside a huge increase in global greenhouse gas emissions. Moreover, although at present the highest CO_2 emissions are coming from China, not the West, if the data is viewed historically and per head of population, the graphics look different:

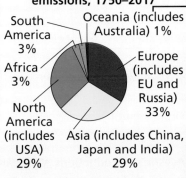

Percentage share of CO_2 emissions, 1750–2017

- Oceania (includes Australia) 1%
- South America 3%
- Africa 3%
- North America (includes USA) 29%
- Asia (includes China, Japan and India) 29%
- Europe (includes EU and Russia) 33%

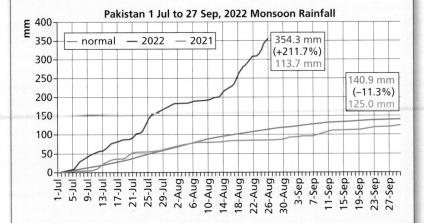

Pakistan 1 Jul to 27 Sep, 2022 Monsoon Rainfall

— normal — 2022 — 2021

354.3 mm (+211.7%) 113.7 mm

140.9 mm (−11.3%) 125.0 mm

I am grateful to Our World in Data for this information, as unbiased evaluation of scientific data is vital in this argument.

Ayesha has chosen an issue which has personal and national impact and makes this clear in her introduction.

Another national perspective is quickly introduced to suggest global consequences.

It would be good to add a paragraph break here.

Vocabulary

hectored: tried to make somebody do something by being aggressive

Ayesha engages with possible bias in both sources.

Ayesha's graphic is dramatic but what does it prove? The assertion that follows needs more evidence to support and explain it. The graph needs more analysis.

Sources: Pakistan Meteorological Department; 'CO2 emissions', Hannah Ritchie and Max Roser, Our World in Data, 2020.

Ayesha acknowledges the source of her data within the text. She could use a footnote.

While it is difficult even for scientists to establish exactly how much the 2022 flooding was caused by greenhouse gas emissions and how much by erratic climate conditions such as La Niña, the link between greenhouse gas emissions and climate change is well established. For example, in the USA the NASA website says the cause of global warming is 'humans interfering with the planet's energy balance'. The history of industrial and economic development in the Global North places a heavy burden on us to act responsibly and set targets to reduce our carbon emissions!

Good choice of another global perspective.

Ayesha has moved from causes to consequences, and from the global to more national concerns.

What are the possible advantages of a plant-based diet and is this practical in Qatar, which imports much of its food?

I am keen on sport and like to eat healthily, but I also care about my planet and about the welfare of animals and wanted to find out more about a plant-based diet, what it means and why people think it is better for us. I have discovered two main reasons for this: it makes less wasteful use of the planet's precious resources and it can contribute to a longer and healthier life. That should be of interest to everyone! The problem with eating meat is that half of all farmed animal emissions come from beef and lamb (Poore and Nemecek 2018) as animals produce methane while digesting and their manure is also a source of methane. The UN's Intergovernmental Panel on climate change claims food contributes to 25% of total global greenhouse gas emissions. Beef production has led to deforestation, which is another cause of climate change, as outlined in the futurelearn website. It requires four times as much water to produce beef as lentils. So, eating a lot of meat damages the planet's vital resources.

The second global reason for eating less meat is that it is healthier...

Kito's lively style makes an easy transition from the personal to the global.

Kito embeds reference to the research he has done.

④ Share your opinions of Kito and Ayesha's introductions. What are their relative strengths and weaknesses? What do they need to do to turn these drafts into final versions?

Ayesha evaluates different viewpoints on the floods first, before looking at how this is a global issue we should all be concerned about. This is a slightly different approach from the model suggested n Unit 5.3, but it fits her material and should work well. Although she has a strong personal commitment to her topic, she has taken care to balance out different perspectives and contrasting explanations of the causes and consequences of flooding and global warming, supported by relevant graphics.

Kito is taking a different approach from Ayesha because he is not comparing two very different perspectives on the same issue but evaluating two main reasons why more plant-based eating would be a good thing. For his argument, he does not need to argue that everyone should be vegan, but simply that a more plant-based diet would be good for the planet and for our own health. He has drawn on arguments that are global both in scale and source, and he is making good use of his research and plan.

Both Ayesha and Kito need to do further evaluation of their sources of information.

5   **a)** Look back at Kito's plan (in Unit 5.5) and review of sources (Unit 5.3). What should he now go on to say about the EAT-Lancet Commission on Food, Planet, Health?

b) How will this help him to evaluate another global perspective on the issue?

c) How will he ensure he has fulfilled the success criteria for the first two paragraphs?

Kito feels he needs a balancing perspective so that his research does not sound too one-sided. He has found this argument on the Fighting Infodemics website:

> Another researcher who studies environmental impacts of food, Joseph Poore from University of Oxford...drew attention to the fact that air-transported fruits and vegetables can generate more GHG emissions per kilogram than chicken, turkey and duck meat.

6   **a)** Why is this a useful perspective for Kito to add?

b) How does it naturally lead on to his national perspective, which is applying the principles of plant-based eating in his international school in Qatar?

> When drafting your report, think about the links and connections you can make between different stages of your argument.

Applying

7 Redraft your own introductory analysis, making sure you have included a clear explanation of causes and consequences.

Follow this with a paragraph evaluating two different global perspectives and make a fair evaluation of their strengths and weaknesses. Check that you have:

- explored different arguments
- explained your reasoning for why you find one or both arguments persuasive.

> **Revising what you have learned**
>
> Unit 2.1 explored how to present different perspectives on the same issue and Unit 4.2 compared global and national perspectives on causes and consequences.

? REFLECTION POINT

In writing your introductory analysis, to what extent have you achieved the following:

- explained the issue for a non-specialist
- presented both factual evidence and reasoning
- evaluated different perspectives in a balanced way?

In your reflective journal, note down the ways in which you have redrafted and changed your introductory analysis in response to verbal feedback from other students, and in response to comparison with the examples here, and from others in your group.

Developing your argument by evaluating different perspectives

Skills focus
✓ Evaluation
✓ Communication

Learning focus
- Give two or more national perspectives.
- Evaluate counterarguments.
- Contrast global and national perspectives.

Big question: How do perspectives differ on this issue?

Getting started

In your plan, evaluating different perspectives forms the main section of your research report. It is especially helpful to have at least two different global perspectives. Your research should also have identified two national perspectives on the issue and possible solutions: the two national perspectives do not need to be from your country and also do not need to be from the same country. However, they should give examples of possible national responses to the global issue.

You will want to compare and contrast these national perspectives with the global perspectives you have chosen: how are they similar and how are they different?

1 Discuss the global and national perspectives on your issue with others on your topic table. Return to the perspectives you noted in the plan and added to your reflective journal. Have you found a good range of different perspectives on the topic?

> A national perspective will look at the appropriateness of action on a global issue in the national context: what is relevant and appropriate in the national context.

Approaching the task

Your research report has a sequence of arguments and ends with your own research and recommendations. In redrafting your work, you will need to evaluate the arguments presented more closely.

2 Bring a written evaluation of one of your competing national perspectives to your group. Share around your topic table.

a) As students' work is passed around the table, annotate it with these symbols:

* an interesting fact or argument

\+ something I would like to know more about: you need to provide more detail

^ this is good, but you need to explain more clearly or concisely

− something I think you have left out (say what it is).

b) Now give each other individual feedback on your arguments.

c) As a table, discuss what you have learned: do your arguments need more facts, clearer explanation, more analysis or more comparison and evaluation?

Evaluating

Remember that it helps your argument to distinguish between two clearly different national perspectives; you need counterarguments for evaluation and you should clarify the difference between global and national perspectives.

3 Kito and Ayesha have been adding national perspectives to the arguments you read in the previous unit. Around your topic table, discuss the two examples that follow.

Indoor farming in Qatar during the summer and winter seasons.

Kito has been looking at how realistic a plant-based diet would be in Qatar, a country which imports most of its food. Because he has a good range of global and national sources, he can make the transition from the global debate to a specific national perspective, illustrated by examples, and suggest a local action.

a) Is there more Kito can do to illustrate his arguments?

Qatar is a country that imports 90% of its food. Much of the country is desert and its growing international urban community, initially drawn to Qatar owing to its rich natural resources, is intensely demanding of natural resources. Food security for Qatar is an urgent issue and is an ambitious priority for its government. The Minister of Municipality has said 'the strategy of agriculture and food security in the country is based on achieving self-sufficiency' (Qatar Tribune 11/03/2022). How does switching to a more plant-based diet help Qatar? In a country that needs to conserve natural resources and reduce emissions, it could make a vital contribution, but only if linked to a reduction in food mileage by continuing to build Qatar's agricultural base. It makes sense to do this through production of fruit and vegetables rather than meat, to contribute both to the national ecosystem and the health of its citizens. For example, the Sahara Forest Project is an exciting project utilising seawater to provide conditions for growing vegetables in greenhouses heated through solar power and using thermal desalination (Suresh, EcoMENA 2022).

We could begin action at a local level, by encouraging two meat-free days a week at our own school. This would only work if we also made greater use of local sources for our food supplies, so as primary research I asked our caterers who supplied our food.

A succinct analysis of the causes and consequences that make Qatar a special case.

The food security strategy is one example to illustrate the national perspective.

This is another, and specific, national example that usefully links diet and climate resilience.

Kito moves fluently from national action to local action.

Ayesha has been looking at national actions in Germany that could reduce carbon emissions to **mitigate** against climate change.

b) Working on your own, annotate Ayesha's response and then summarise its strengths and weaknesses.

Vocabulary

mitigate: make something less serious

> Germany, where I live, can make an important contribution to fixing the historic imbalance of contributions to global warming between Global North and Global South if it can meet its ambitious targets for renewable energy. A national climate law was passed in 2019, and in 2020 the country overshot its target to increase energy emissions by 40%. However, this was partly due to the pandemic, and calculations for 2021 look less favourable (CleanEnergyWire). In March 2022, it was announced that Germany, as Europe's largest economy, had released 4.5% more CO_2 in 2021, mainly due to increased emissions from the energy sector, as reported on the Bloomberg news website, a depressing statistic for those who want to see the country meet its targets. The Pakistan floods are a reminder of the global consequences of falling short of national targets. According to the German government, two changes will be critical: phasing out coal in favour of renewables, especially wind power, for electricity generation and restructuring mobility with greener energy for transport (bundesregierung website). At an individual level, everyone could help by rethinking their energy and transport needs.
>
> A survey in our own international school on how to reduce our carbon footprint through changes to transport, heating and lighting came up with interesting results about how local action can contribute to global needs.

Working through the success criteria for this section of the research report, Ayesha:

- identifies and gives examples of a national perspective on climate change

- begins to evaluate the causes and consequences of Germany missing its targets in 2021 – she could look at this in more detail

- compares global and national perspectives, making a link to her earlier work on the Pakistan floods

- clearly identifies two areas for action, and makes effective links between national concerns and specific local actions

- shows good skills of synthesis (bringing together arguments from different sources) based on her research

- could explore sources of information in more detail, either in the body of her essay or in her critical bibliography (this point also applies to Kito's report).

Applying

Here is a reminder of what is expected in this section of your report. This will bring together the material in your plan, synthesising arguments into a clear evaluation of national perspectives based on more than one viewpoint.

Evaluating and analysing national perspectives	Give two examples and an analysis of national causes and consequences for your chosen country.	200 words

4 Now write up the evaluation section of your research report. Make sure you have explained at least two different national perspectives on the issue, supported by examples.

a) Explain how these national perspectives differ.

b) Compare these with global perspectives on the issue.

c) Provide more analysis of causes and consequences of different perspectives on the issue.

d) Come to your own conclusions about the perspective you want to prioritise in order to find a solution to the problem.

Revising what you have learned

....

Unit 4.3 evaluated different arguments about cycle helmets, Unit 2.4 modelled evaluating a source in close detail and Unit 2.5 looked at using data to support arguments.

❓ REFLECTION POINT

• How do different perspectives help you to come to your own conclusion about a recommended action?

• Has reading about different perspectives changed or developed your thinking about the issue?

• How does the relationship between national and global perspectives help you to formulate a realistic local action?

Make a note in your reflective journal (which should be dated) to show the process through which your thinking has developed.

Revising what you have learned

....

Remember it is OK to change your mind! To see an example of this, look again at Unit 3.5, which shows reflection based on research. Different perspectives can change your own thinking, and you will be asked to reflect on your learning at the end of your report.

Making a recommendation for action

Skills focus
✓ Analysis
Learning focus
- Recommend an appropriate course of action.
- Explain how it will be carried out.
- Explain its possible consequences.

Big question: What is your solution to the problem?

Approaching the task

The last section of the write-up is your recommendation. This is your SMART target for local action that you identified earlier and tested through primary research.

You should already have a realistic target for local or national action. You need to support this with evidence that it could achieve something that helps to solve a global problem. Your primary research should help you to establish how much support there is for your proposed solution.

1 Make sure you have clear support for the perspective you present as your final course of action.

a) Copy and complete a chart like the one below to help clarify this.

Recommended course of action	
Factual evidence that supports it	
Reasoning by others that supports it (your secondary research)	
Your own reasoning and personal perspective	
Why the action is achievable	
Relevant evidence from your primary research that it is realistic and supported by others	
Suggested timeframe for action	
How the action can solve both global and national problems	

b) Check your proposal with a partner. Can they understand your reasoning and do they agree that it is realistic?

Evaluating

Your final task is to write up your recommendation.

First, read these two different approaches to making recommendations for action.

- Kito is recommending that his school have two meat-free days per week to promote a plant-based diet.

- Ayesha is recommending further action for climate change in Germany.

2 As you read, consider which recommendation is better supported by evidence and more likely to be effective. Note down the reasons for your views.

My research revealed the benefits of plant-based diets both for personal health and for the planet. The EAT-Lancet Commission showed how emissions could be cut by up to 80%, and we could reduce the risk of developing cardiovascular diseases. Eating more fruit and vegetables will also help us to meet Qatar's food security targets. For our meat-free days at school, it was crucial to find out how our food was sourced, so I interviewed the catering manager. She directed me to the Unilever website, for the multinational brands we often use and their sustainable development goals, but she had not heard of the Sahara Forest Project so agreed to source local produce. We realised that talking to the Principal and publicising my idea was crucial. With her agreement, we sent out questionnaires to all Stage 9 students with information on what meat-free days would achieve for the planet and for personal health. 70% of students agreed. With staff and student support, we trialled two meat-free days with other Stage 9 students as ambassadors for change. I hope we can make that local change a permanent one, and also contribute to global and national awareness of food origins and impact.

Evidence-based conclusions.

More reasoning based on research.

Primary research makes the plan realistic.

Link to comment bubble above.

Specific and time-related trial.

Kito sets out evidence-based local action that is specific and realistic. He has also ensured there is enough support to make it achievable.

I felt as a school community we could do more to achieve our national emission reduction target and spoke to my teacher, who suggested I interview the Operations Manager of the school. They detailed the costs of heating and lighting the school, and of school transport. I then did an attitudes survey of school students and discovered that 10% of students who travelled to school by car did so in an electric vehicle, only 15% of students walked or cycled to school and most travelled on school coaches. I seriously recommend that students look at their personal energy use and transport to school and ask if their journeys could be made in a more carbon neutral way.

Although Ayesha has excellent ideas, she needs to do more to ensure others share her goals.

- She could add more research to support her targets for the school and use the statistics from the Operations Manager to make them specific and achievable.

- Rather than trying to change the way students travel to school, it might be more realistic to find ways to encourage them to switch off lights, power down devices when not in use and make fewer demands on the heating system. The survey is potentially a good way to achieve agreement about those goals, if they are SMART and well-informed.

Final task

3 Now, write up the conclusion of your report: it should be a clear recommendation for action that can solve national problems at a realistic local level.

Proposing a solution	What has your own research shown? Set out a specific and realistic national or local action that could help to solve the problem.	150–200 words, including use of evidence, reasoning and explanation of why it is an achievable goal.

Revising what you have learned

Units 4.5 and 4.6 show you how to make recommendations based on research into your local community and its needs or preferences.

4 Share your conclusion with another member of your topic group.

- Do they agree that this is a sensible course of action?
- Is it well-reasoned and supported by evidence?
- What do you think about their own solution?

Use 'three stars and a wish' to give some positive feedback to each other.

Then redraft your conclusion to include the wish, while checking that you are remaining within the word limit.

❓ REFLECTION POINT

- Why should reports end with recommendations for action?
- How has the issue now been explored at a global, national and local level?
- Have you ensured that each perspective is supported by evidence and reasoning?
- How persuasive are your recommendations to others?

Write a note in your reflective journal about how happy you are about your final recommendation and what you have done to ensure it is achievable.

Look back over your reflective journal. What have you learned about the process of problem solving and communicating your evaluation and conclusions to others?

Add a couple of sentences about the skills you have learned in drawing conclusions from your research.

Proofreading, checking and referencing your final report

Skills focus
✓ Communication

Learning focus
• Ensure that arguments are well-reasoned and structured.
• Check in-text citations and referencing of sources.

Big question: How do you improve your final draft?

Approaching the task

1 **a)** Make sure you have a readable and accessible first draft and bring your print-out to class or upload it to a shared workspace.

b) Swap drafts with a critical partner from your topic group. When marking each other's drafts, you can point out where the writer's ideas or expression are unclear, although you must not correct their work or add to it: the corrections are for the writer to make. Use the 'Checklist for success' to guide you.

c) Discuss your feedback with your partner.

Using subheadings for different stages of your report can also help with the clarity of your argument and demonstrate that you have met the brief you were set. The subheadings should not be about the content but the skills and perspectives you are highlighting.

The word limits included in the table below are guidelines and the section headings are suggestions. You must not exceed the total word limit of 1000 words, including footnotes and bibliography.

Checklist for success

Proofreading your partner's draft:

✔ Underline or highlight areas that are unclear.

✔ Look out for errors in:

  ✔ spelling

  ✔ punctuation

  ✔ grammar

  ✔ sentence construction.

✔ Errors should be highlighted but not corrected.

Section heading	Content	Word limit
Title	Your question	20 words
Analysis of the issue	What is the problem and why is it a problem?	250 words
Evaluating global perspectives	What should we all be doing about this issue in the future?	200 words
Evaluating and analysing national perspectives	Give two examples and an analysis of national causes and consequences for your chosen country.	200 words
Proposing a solution	A local or national goal	200 words

2 **a)** Check that your report is clearly subdivided and presented. Each section should:

• be divided into paragraphs

• have a clear argument

• include references to the sources used.

b) Ask another critical partner from your topic group to look at your report's paragraphing, subheadings and clarity of presentation. You will review these elements of their report.

c) Share feedback and listen to any suggestions for improvement.

Applying

Referencing must be embedded within your argument. This can be done through:

- in-text citation (including a name and date in brackets in the body of your text), OR

- footnoting (with a full reference at the bottom of the page).

URLs of websites used can be pasted into a footnote; they should not appear in the body of the text.

Both forms of referencing need to be followed by a full citation of your source in your bibliography.

3 **a)** Make sure any statements that are not your own are placed within quotations.

    b) Check that each quotation is followed by a reference that clearly identifies the source you used.

    c) Make sure your reference is followed by analysis of the perspective you are citing. Is it a global or a national perspective? Is it credible and reliable? How has it helped to develop your own thinking?

4 Swap draft assignments and check a partner's work using the 'Checklist for success'. Can you follow up the URLs they have provided for internet sources? Highlight anything they need to clarify and improve, then discuss what you have found together.

> **Revising what you have learned**
> ....
> Unit 4.4 explained the importance of referencing and gave examples of footnoting and in-text citation.

Final task

5 Carry out a final review of your final draft using the 'Checklist'.

Checklist for success
....

✔ Are you within the word limit for each section?

✔ Is the spelling accurate, do sentences make sense, is punctuation in the right place?

✔ Have you written short, clear paragraphs and used subheadings?

✔ Are all statements that are not your own placed within quotations?

✔ Is each quotation followed by a reference that clearly identifies the source used?

✔ Do you refer to the skills you show and the perspectives you explore?

> **❓ REFLECTION POINT**
> In your reflective journal, comment on what you have learned about communication from the process of proofreading, checking and referencing your final report.

Providing a critical bibliography

Skills focus
✓ Evaluation

Learning focus
• Present a range of sources correctly.
• Evaluate their credibility.

Big question: How do you formally record the sources used?

Getting started

Referencing is very important. All your work needs to be your own. If you are citing the words, factual information or arguments of others, you must reference these. You need in-text citations, either in the body of your report or in footnotes, and a bibliography at the end that lists them all in alphabetical order. You can turn this into a critical bibliography by adding a brief comment to show you have evaluated the source of information.

1 Bring a list of your references to your topic table and discuss how you can comment concisely on the way you have used them, explaining this to others.

Exploring

You began your research by finding different arguments about the issue or problem and you developed your research by looking at different possible solutions. You looked at the problems of implementing a solution to a global problem at a local or national level and why there are arguments for and against taking specific actions. You should have kept a record of the sources you have used in your reflective journal and used these to reference the arguments you have evaluated.

2 Consider the best ways to list your sources. Discuss these questions with a partner from your topic group.

a) Why do we list sources alphabetically by the author's surname?

b) Why are publication dates important?

c) Why do we need to make sure that the URLs of web pages used still work?

Here is an example of how to list in a bibliography:

> Surname, Initial (year of publication/presentation), 'Title of item', Title of publication [italics] [If accessed online:] Available at: URL (Accessed: date).
>
> If there is no named author, cite the organisation, for example:
>
> WHO (2022), 'State of the world's drinking water: an urgent call to action to accelerate progress on ensuring safe drinking water for all' Available at: https://www.who.int/publications/i/item/9789240060807 (Accessed 29/09/2022)

3 Now reorganise your references alphabetically. You will use these as the basis for the bibliography at the end of your report.

Developing

Before you add a brief evaluative comment to each item in your bibliography, look at how Ayesha and Kito comment on sources in their critical bibliographies. Both are using a simplified referencing system to give credit to the authors of the website articles they have used.

(Appunn, Eriksen, Wettengle 2021), 'Germany's greenhouse gas emissions and energy transition targets': Factsheet on cleanenergywire website.

This review of evidence by journalists is funded by the Stiftung Mercator and European Climate Change Foundation and reviews Germany's progress towards its goals. They conclude that Germany is very successful in developing renewals but less so in reducing energy demand, which requires everyone to participate.

(Umweltbundesamt, 2022) https://www.umweltbundesamt.de/en/data/environmental-indicators/indicator-greenhouse-gas-emissions#at-a-glance [published 15.3.2022]

Website of Germany's main environmental protection agency, which advises the government and confirms that Germany missed its targets in 2021.

(Infodemics, 2021) 'Can going vegan help to solve our environmental problems?' https://infodemics.blog/2021/07/07/can-going-vegan-help-to-solve-our-environmental-problems/

I wanted a counterargument about vegan diets. This is an interesting blog as it is evidence-based and aims to debunk misconceptions, although the author is anonymous.

---

4   Compare the strengths and weaknesses of the two students' reports.

Final task

5   Complete the critical bibliography for your research project. Make sure you have included all the sources for the facts and arguments you have presented. Ensure these are referenced correctly.

Support your references with a brief evaluative comment about the author's expertise, the purpose and reliability of the argument and whether it is supported by evidence from other sources.

> **? REFLECTION POINT**
>
> - Checking over your work, do your facts, argument, references and bibliography match?
>
> - Do you have a range of different perspectives?
>
> - Do you have evidence from different countries?
>
> - Are you confident that you have evaluated the purpose and possible bias of the sources you have used?
>
> In your reflective journal, note what you have learned through the process of checking and evaluating your source material.

Explaining how your personal perspective has changed as a result of research

Big question: What difference has my research made to me?

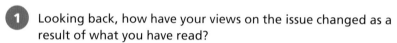

Getting started

At the beginning of the process of planning your research report, you chose an issue related to one of the topic areas in the Global Perspectives syllabus. The research you have done should have helped you to investigate current global problems and suggest future solutions.

1 Looking back, how have your views on the issue changed as a result of what you have read?

Go back over your reflective journal and then discuss with a partner.

Exploring

Even if your perspective has not changed as a result of encountering other arguments and viewpoints, it should have deepened and developed.

To write a successful personal reflection on the issue you will need to:

• make reference to the research you have conducted

• relate to a national or global perspective you have analysed.

Remember that perspectives are characterised by their use of evidence and reasoning, so each stage of the development of your personal perspective should be mapped with factual evidence and with an argument from that evidence. That way, you can chart what you have discovered and what difference that has made.

2 a) Copy and complete the following planning grid:

Stage of my research	Reasoning	Evidence	Effect on my personal perspective on the issue
What I thought about the issue at the start of my research			
A fact or piece of information I discovered through research that changed or developed my thinking			
An argument I found that changed or developed my thinking			

How analysing a perspective made me understand it better			
How my thoughts and understanding of the issue have developed			

b) When you have completed the grid, spend a minute explaining how your perspective developed to the rest of your group.

c) How confident did you feel about explaining what you have learned? Did you support it with examples?

Developing

Good reflection needs specific reference both to what you learned and to what deeper analysis of arguments has revealed.

3 Here are Ayesha's and Kito's reflection paragraphs. Which do you think meets the success criteria in the planning grid better and why?

My thinking about climate change was provoked by the news stories about Pakistan and as this is a global issue, I wanted to explore the causes and consequences from a Western perspective at home in Germany. I was surprised to find that not everyone agrees that global warming is to blame for the flooding and discovered the issue is more complex than I thought at first. But what was most disappointing was to discover that even though here in Germany we care a lot about the environment, our greenhouse emissions have gone up since the end of the global pandemic. It's as if we haven't learned! It was good to research ways we could make a difference in our own school community by discussing our energy use with school staff and surveying attitudes to transport among my classmates.

I liked the idea of encouraging plant-based eating because I want to be kinder to animals and to the planet. In my research, I discovered a lot about how plant-based diets can reduce carbon emissions and make you live longer! I discovered how Qatar is encouraging greater food self-sufficiency and growing fruit and vegetables more sustainably. This helped me to think how our school could make a difference if we found out more about where our food comes from. By putting out information in my survey I found I could encourage other students to eat in a healthier and more environmental way.

Final task: the reflection

4 Add a further paragraph to conclude your report with a personal reflection on the topic you have researched. You should write around 100 words. Consider:

- How has the process of researching information, analysing the issue, evaluating the perspectives and recommending action developed your understanding of global and national perspectives on the topic?

- Have you changed your view?

- Have you discovered something new?

- Have any perspectives on the subject surprised you or challenged you?

Draw on your reflective journal entries as well as the planning grid in this unit.

> **Revising what you have learned**
> ....
> Unit 4.7 gives you examples of how to conclude a report with personal reflection.

5 Share your personal reflection with a partner in your topic group for feedback and then make any changes you need.

Reflecting on skills development and targets for improvement

Big question: What have I learned about myself as a student?

Getting started

1 **a)** Remind yourself of the key skills taught in Global Perspectives:

> Analysis   Collaboration   Communication
> Evaluation   Reflection   Research

b) Which of these skills have you practised most in compiling your research report? Organise the skills in the order of highest to lowest priority in completing the report.

Exploring

2 Look back over your reflective journal and notes for your report, as well as the draft report itself.

a) Find examples of where you have practised the six key skills taught in Global Perspectives. Copy and complete the chart below, and add your examples to the first column.

	Examples	Strengths	Opportunities
I researched when I....			
I analysed when I...			
I evaluated when I...			
I communicated when I...			
I collaborated when I...			
I reflected when I...			

b) Go back over each of these examples. Consider:

- What went well?

- What could have been better?

- What did you learn from working on your own on an issue you had chosen?

- What did you learn from communicating with others working in the same topic area?

- How would you summarise your strengths and where did you find opportunities to improve?

c) Add your thoughts to the 'Strengths' and 'Opportunities' columns of the chart. Make sure you include specific examples in the rows relating to each of the six skills.

Developing

Kito and Ayesha have each written around 60 words on what they have learned through writing their research reports.

3 Read through Ayesha's and Kito's self-evaluation statements. Which is stronger and why?

My research involved discovering different global perspectives on what caused climate change. I analysed the causes and consequences of flooding in Pakistan, evaluated which sources were most reliable and collaborated with my school community through an interview and survey to find out what we could do to reduce our carbon footprint. I communicated and reflected through my report.

Ayesha has set out the process but not really reflected on her personal skills development.

I enjoyed finding out the different ways in which plant-based diets help us and the planet and deepened my evaluation by discovering that food miles matter as well as food content, especially here in Qatar. My communication skills improved greatly by redrafting, footnoting and editing my report, so that it made a clear argument for the difference we could make through well-informed meat-free days.

Kito is good at linking what he has done to the development of his skills and making connections between his own skills and the message he wants to communicate to others.

Final task

4 Write a self-evaluation statement of what you have learned about your study skills on the Stage 9 Global Perspectives course, and especially when planning and writing up your own research report. This statement forms the final part of your reflection.

This is not part of the formal research report or your summative assessment, but it is a useful review of how your skills have developed. You should write between 50 and 100 words.

5 Your final report will now have arguments, information, evidence and reasoning under the following subheadings:

Title	Ensure you have included your name and teaching group, your choice of topic and the question.	Word limit: 20 words
Introductory analysis	Analyse the causes and consequences of the global issue: what is the problem and why is it a problem?	250 words
Evaluating global perspectives	Evaluate a global perspective commenting on use of evidence and why the perspective is global: what should we all be doing about this issue in the future?	200 words
Evaluating and analysing national perspectives	Give two or more examples to support a national perspective on this issue and explain the differences between global and national perspectives. What solution would be appropriate for your chosen country or region?	200 words
Proposing a solution	What has your own research shown? Set out a specific and realistic national or local action which could help to solve the problem.	200 words
Reflection on the issue	Explain how your personal perspective has changed.	50–100 words
Self-evaluation	Explain what you have learned from the project: this will be additional to your report and is a showcase for how your skills have developed.	Not included in final report.

Checklist for success

Finalising your research report

✔ Make sure all your subheadings are in the correct places.

✔ Check you are within the word limits: the total length of the report must not exceed 1000 words and should not be fewer than 800 words.

✔ Check the spelling, formatting and presentation of your report. Ask someone from another group who has never read your work before to check it for clarity of English and expression.

You are now ready to submit your final report!

❓ REFLECTION POINT

How has writing a research report deepened your understanding of what Global Perspectives really are and what it means to think globally and act locally?

Your school could hold a Global Perspectives event in which you share your reports with younger students or with parents and explain what you gained from doing individual research. Bring along extracts from your notebook, reflective journal, posters, information flyers and any other visual support for your research such as photos or short video clips.

Check your progress

Beginning	Developing	Going beyond
• I can choose a question and identify a cause or consequence of a global issue.	• I can formulate a relevant research question and analyse causes and consequences.	• I can formulate a well-constructed and focused question and explain causes and consequences in some detail.
• I can evaluate a source of information and comment on its use of evidence.	• I can evaluate at least one source of information and recognise bias.	• I can evaluate sources of information, explaining why some are biased.
• I can give an example that supports a national perspective on the issue.	• I can present and explain at least one national perspective on the issue.	• I can present a clear national perspective on the issue supported by at least two examples.
• I can propose a local action to address the global problem.	• I can propose a local action that may help resolve the issue.	• I can propose a local action that is likely to resolve the issue.
• I can reflect on how my personal perspective has changed.	• I can reflect on how my personal perspective has developed or changed with reference to research and evidence.	• I can reflect on how my personal perspective has developed or changed with reference to the research I have conducted and the perspectives I have analysed.

Next steps

- What other global issues might be addressed through specific local actions in your country or community? Share your projects as a class or year group, showcase them with the school community of parents, teachers and other classes, and consider inviting local representatives to hear your ideas.

- How has your understanding of the way different perspectives are presented and supported by evidence changed as a result of this course? Has your work on Global Perspectives changed where you go to find information and the way you check arguments when you read about them?

Glossary of key terms

argument: a series of statements containing reasons and evidence which support a claim about a global issue

assumption: something accepted as true without proof

bias: an inbuilt prejudice

biased: unfairly prejudiced for or against something or someone

causal link: a relationship based on causation

causation: when one thing causes another

closed questions: questions with a limited or set range of responses, for example: 'Do you own a mobile phone?'

cluster: a group of closely linked figures or examples

control group: research group that is not exposed to the experimental factor being tested

correlation: relationship between two sets of data or between two variables

counterevidence: facts or information that supports an alternative viewpoint

credible: reasonable or believable, for example whether the evidence comes from a reputable source

empirical: based on observation or experience

emotive language: language that appeals to a reader's emotions

et al.: abbreviation meaning 'and others', used to indicate when a source text has more than one author

expertise: specialist knowledge or skills

extrapolate: work out from evidence, assuming its indications will remain consistent

fact-checked: a key element of responsible news media is that any claims and statistics are fact-checked by in-house teams and lawyers to avoid false claims and 'fake news'

flawed: based on a false logic

footnotes: a method of referencing sources where the details appear at the foot of the page

imperative: a command or instruction

infographic: information displayed in an interesting way visually

mean average: the total of all scores divided between the number of scores; for example, if six students give scores of 5, 6, 6, 8, 6, 5, the mean average is 36 ÷ 6, which is 6

modifying factors: factors that will create changes in the data

multiple choice: questions that provide a set number of given responses to choose from, for example: 'How do you use your phone for educational purposes?' A: internet for homework, B: revision apps, C: calculator, D: other

open questions: questions that generate a range of answers with no defined length, for example: 'How do you feel if you have to spend time without your phone?'

peer-reviewed: the peer review process is important to academic publication, and involves checking the validity of the research and its claims by other academics working in the field before publication

perspective: a viewpoint on an issue based on evidence and reasoning

plagiarism: using or presenting someone else's work as if it were your own

spread: distribution of data

standard deviation: a measure of how dispersed the data is in relation to the mean average

synthesis: combining ideas or points into a new text

trend: a general development in the way something happens; a pattern in data

unbiased: lacking prejudice, fair

valid: acceptable in terms of relevance and timing, etc.

variable: characteristic, factor or quantity that can increase or decrease

verifiable: able to be checked as accurate or true

vested interest: having a stake in the issue, for example gaining financially from it

Acknowledgements

Texts

We are grateful to the following for permission to reproduce copyright material. In some instances, we have been unable to trace the owners of copyright material, and we would appreciate any information that would enable us to do so.

Figures 1.2.3 and 1.2.4, pp.8–9, 'Prevalence of Key TB Risk factors (and 95% Confidence Interval) by wealth level' and 'Self Reported TB prevalence (per 100,000) by wealth quintile' in *Tuberculosis and Poverty: Why Are the Poor at Greater Risk in India?* by Olivia Oxlade and Megan Murray, PLoS One. 2012; 7(11): e47533. https://www.ncbi.nlm.nih.gov/pmc/articles/PMC3501509/ Figures 1, 2, copyright © Oxlade, Murray, 2012. Creative Commons Attribution License; Figure 1.3.1, p.10 'TB mortality rate in Great Britain altered between 1860 and 1950' by Wayne LaMorte, MD, PhD, MP, from *The Sanitary Idea (1850-1875)*, https://sphweb.bumc.bu.edu/otlt/MPH-Modules/EP/EP713_History/EP713_History7.html, Boston University School of Public Health. Reproduced by permission; The data in Figure 1.3.2, p.10 'Why did people fall ill with TB in 2021?', *Summary of tuberculosis data* https://worldhealthorg.shinyapps.io/tb_profiles/ l. Generated by the World Health Organization (WHO), accessed November 2022. Reproduced with permission; The poster on p.14, 'World Blood Donor Day', https://www.who.int/multi-media/details/world-blood-donor-day-poster, WHO, accessed November 2022. Reproduced with permission; An extract on pp.29–30 from 'Delivering education to refugee children through digital,' Children on the Edge, www.childrenontheedge.org. Reproduced with permission; The article title on p.33 'Mobile learning during Covid-19: One-to-one instruction through phone calls can be effective when schooling is disrupted' by Noam Angrist, *The Kathmandu Post*, 24/07/2022, https://kathmandupost.com/columns/2022/07/24/mobile-learning-during-covid-19; The article title on p.33 '10 Advantages to allowing kids to have Cell Phones in Schools' by Thomas Jones, *Wondershare*, 2011, https://famisafe.wondershare.com/monitor/allowing-kids-to-have-cell-phones-in-schools.html; Extracts on pp.36–37 from 'Banning mobile phones in schools can improve students' academic performance. This is how we know' by Louis-Philippe Beland, *The Conversation*, 21/03/2021. https://theconversation.com/banning-mobile-phones-in-schools-can-improve-students-academic-performance-this-is-how-we-know-153792; Figure 2.5.1 on p.41 'In many emerging economies, younger people lead the way in smartphones ownership' by Laura Silver from *Smartphone Ownership Is Growing Rapidly Around the World, but Not Always Equally,* PEW Research Center, 05/02/2019, https://www.pewresearch.org/global/2019/02/05/smartphone-ownership-is-growing-rapidly-around-the-world-but-not-always-equally/. Source; Spring 2018 Global Attitudes Survey, Q46; The article title on p.46 'When education goes all digital, students without smartphones fall behind' by Renuka Bisht, *Times of India*, 09/04/2020, https://timesofindia.indiatimes.com/blogs/twinkle-twinkle/when-education-goes-all-digital-students-without-smartphones-fall-behind/; Figure 3.3.1, p.58, SPM.2 from IPCC, 2014: Summary for Policymakers. In: *Climate Change 2014: Mitigation of Climate Change. Contribution of Working Group III to the Fifth Assessment Report of the Intergovernmental Panel on Climate Change* by O. Edenhofer, R. Pichs-Madruga, Y. Sokona, E. Farahani, S. Kadner, K. Seyboth, A. Adler, I. Baum, S. Brunner, P. Eickemeier, B. Kriemann, J. Savolainen, S. Schlömer, C. von Stechow, T. Zwickel and J.C. Minx (eds.). Cambridge University Press, Cambridge, United Kingdom and New York, NY, USA. Reproduced by permission of IPCC; Figure 3.3.2, p.58 'A European Strategy for low-emission mobility' from *Transport emissions,* https://climate.ec.europa.eu/eu-action/transport-emissions_en, copyright © European Union, 1995-2022. Data source EEA European Environment Agency; Figure 3.3.3, p.59 'Croydon to Wimbledon, 2021 (KgCO2e)' from *Transport and environment statistics: Autumn 2021,* Department for Transport, https://www.gov.uk/government/statistics/transport-and-environment-statistics-autumn-2021/transport-and-environment-statistics-autumn-2021, © Crown copyright, Open Government Licence v3.0; Extracts on pp.79, 88 from 'Why cycling is great for your legs, lungs, immune system and mind, plus 11 other great benefits of life on two wheels!' by Michelle Arthurs-Brennan, Cycling Weekly, 18/11/2022, https://www.cyclingweekly.com/news/latest-news/benefits-of-cycling-334144. Reproduced by permission of Future Publishing; Extract on p.82 from 'Why is physical activity important for child development?', SportSG – Active Health, https://www.activehealth.sg/read/physical-activity/why-is-physical-activity-important-for-child-development. Reproduced with permission; A statistic on p.83 from 'How do children travel to school in urban India? A cross-sectional study of 5,842 children in Hyderabad', *BMC Public Health*, Vol. 16, 1099, 2016. Creative Commons Attribution 4.0 International License; A statistic and infographic on p.83 from

'National Travel Survey 2014: Travel to school', Department of Transport, © Crown copyright; An extract on p.86 from *Richard's New Bicycle Book* by Richard Ballantine, Pan Macmillan, 1990. Reproduced by permission of the Licensor through PLSClear; An extract on p.87 from 'Head injuries and bicycle helmet laws' by D. L. Robinson in *Accident Analysis & Prevention*, Elsevier, Vol. 28, Issue 4, July 1996, pp.463–475, copyright © Elsevier, 1996; An extract on p.90 from 'Walking and cycling good for health even in cities with higher levels of air pollution' in *Preventive Medicine,* University of Cambridge, 05/05/2016. Creative Commons Attribution 4.0 International License; The chart on p.90 'Global CO2 emissions from transport' from *Cars, planes, trains: where do CO2 emissions from transport come from?* 06/10/2020, https://ourworldindata.org/co2-emissions-from-transport. Based on International Energy Agency (IEA) and the International Council on Clean Transportation (ICCT); An extract on p.93 from 'An Intervention to Reduce Bicycle Injuries among Middle School Students in Rural China', *International Journal of Environmental Research and Public Health*, Vol. 14, Issue 7, July 2017, p.690, https://www.ncbi.nlm.nih.gov/pmc/articles/PMC5551128/. Creative Commons Attribution (CC BY) license; An extract on p.94 from *Kids Walk-to-School: A Guide to Promote Walking to School*, National Center for Chronic Disease Prevention and Health Promotion (U.S.), Division of Nutrition and Physical Activity, 2000, https://stacks.cdc.gov/view/cdc/11316, p.19 Reference to specific commercial products, manufacturers, companies, or trademarks does not constitute its endorsement or recommendation by the U.S. Government, Department of Health and Human Services, or Centers for Disease Control and Prevention. Available for free via the agency website; An extract on p.95 from 'Safe Routes to School National Partnership, 2018', Safe Routes Partnership, www.saferotuespartnership. Reproduced with permission; An extract on p.102 from 'The Other Malaysia: A trek through forest to reach school' by Carolyn Hong, *The Straits Times*, 09/02/2015 https://www.straitstimes.com/asia/se-asia/a-trek-through-forest-to-reach-school. Reproduced with permission; Figure 4.7.1, p.103 'Average support for Government Ensuring well-being of the people in the Americas, 2008' from *To What Extent Should Government Ensure Citizen Well-Being?* by Margarita Corral, https://www.vanderbilt.edu/lapop/insights/I0816en_v2.pdf, copyright © LAPOP, 'Insights' series, 2009. Reproduced with permission; Extracts on pp.114–115, 123, 124 from 'Is eating meat bad for the environment?' by Fran, *Future Learn*, 11/05/2021, https://www.futurelearn.com/info/blog/eating-meat-bad-for-environment. Sourced from 'Future Food: Sustainable Food Systems for the 21st Century', University of Exeter. Reproduced with permission from FutureLearn and University of Exeter; and data on p.127 from 'Who has contributed most to global CO2 emissions?' in 'CO2 and Greenhouse Gas emissions' by Hannah Ritchie, Max Roser and Pablo Rosado, Our World in Data, 2020, https://ourworldindata.org/co2-emissions. Data sourced from The Global Carbon Project (GCP) and Carbon Dioxide Analysis Center (CDIAC). Creative Commons BY Licence.

Images

p.1 Maksim Shmeljov/Shutterstock, p.2 Romariolen/Shutterstock, p.3 seaonweb/Shutterstock, p.4 Puwadol Jaturawutthichai/Shutterstock, p.5 Matej Kastelic/Shutterstock, p.7 ViDI Studio/Shutterstock, p.9 Africa Studio/Shutterstock, p.11 Wandering views/Shutterstock, p.12 Yusnizam Yusof/Shutterstock, p.13 Kdonmuang/Shutterstock, p.14 The poster on p.14, World Blood Donor Day, https://www.who.int/multi-media/details/world-blood-donor-day-poster, WHO, accessed November 2022. Reproduced with permission, p.16 Alexander Raths/Shutterstock, p.17 Sunshine Seeds/Shutterstock, p.18 MONOPOLY919/Shutterstock, p.19 Ground Picture/Shutterstock, p.20 Jamie McBean/Shutterstock, p.21 chalermphon_tiam/Shutterstock, p.23 WESTOCK PRODUCTIONS/Shutterstock, p.24 TomWang/shutterstock, p.25 Ground Picture/Shutterstock, p.26 Ground Picture/Shutterstock, p.27 Studiofy.de/Shutterstock, p.27 jordaneil/Shutterstock, p.27 Supachita Krerkkaiwan/Shutterstock , p.28 Michal Knitl/shutterstock, pp.29–30 'Digital education for Rohingya refugee children in Kutupalong camp, Bangladesh', © Children on the Edge; p.30 chaylek/Shutterstock, p.32 ASDF_MEDIA/shutterstock, p.35 DELBO ANDREA/Shutterstock, p.36 Vilnis Karklins/shutterstock, p.37 SpeedKingz/shutterstock, p.38 Joseph Sohm/Shutterstock, p.38 Daniele COSSU/Shutterstock, p.40 Pheelings media/Shutterstock, p.44 Rido/Shutterstock, p.45 POP-THAILAND/Shutterstock, p.46 Odua Images/Shutterstock, p.47 Ground Picture/Shutterstock, p.49 akimovkonstantin/shutterstock, p.50 Mazur Travel Guide/shutterstock, p.50 PradeepGaurs/shutterstock, p.50 effectivestockphotos/shutterstock, p.51 Roman Zaiets/shutterstock, p.51 Paolo Bona/shutterstock, p.52 Ground Picture/Shutterstock, p.53 Robert Kneschke/shutterstock, p.55 Unique Vision/shutterstock, p.55 xuanhuongho/shutterstock, p.55 David Fuentes Prieto/shutterstock, p.55 Albert Pego/Shutterstock, p.56 Wirestock Creators/Shutterstock, p.56 Anna Om/shutterstock, pp.58-59 metoffice/what-is-climate-change, p.60 SM AKBAR ALI PJ/shutterstock, p.61 Olaf Speier/Shutterstock, p.62 Odua Images/shutterstock, p.63 lunamarina/shutterstock, p.64 cowardlion/shutterstock, p.65 ESB Professional/Shutterstock, p.66 Dusan Petkovic/shutterstock, p.66 EQRoy/shutterstock, p.66 EQRoy/shutterstock, p.67 Odua Images/

shutterstock, p.68 kurhan/shutterstock, p.68 Roman Chazov/shutterstock, p.70 Pressmaster/shutterstock, p.71 Sven Hansche/shutterstock, p.71 ventdusud/shutterstock, p.71 Sorbis/shutterstock, p.73 Rawpixel. com/Shutterstock, p.75 Firmansyah Asep/Shutterstock, p.76 Kekyalyaynen/Shutterstock, p.78 WESTOCK PRODUCTIONS/shutterstock, p.79 Jimmy Kamballur/shutterstock, p.80 Casa nayafana/shutterstock, p.80 AlessandroBiascioli/shutterstock, p.82 Rawpixel.com/shutterstock, p.83 Shchus/shutterstock, p.84 Rawpixel.com/shutterstock, p.85 Lopolo/shutterstock, p.86 Odua Images/shutterstock, p.88 AlessandroBiascioli/shutterstock, p.89 Michaelpuche/shutterstock, p.90 lzf/shutterstock, p.91 dotshock/ shutterstock, p.92 Natee Meepian/shutterstock, p.94 James Jiao/shutterstock, p.95 Jaren Jai Wicklund/ shutterstock, p.96 Monkey Business Images/shutterstock, p.98 Robert Kneschke/shutterstock, p.99 Sophon Nawit/shutterstock, p.100 Kumpol Vashiraaskorn/shutterstock, p.101 LightField Studios/shutterstock, p.102 Lano Lan/shutterstock, p.105 Sudarshan Jha/Shutterstock, p.107 Ground Picture/Shutterstock, p.108 Rawpixel.com/Shutterstock, p.109 SpeedKingz/Shutterstock, p.110 pickingpok/Shutterstock, p.111 Asianet-Pakistan/Shutterstock, p.112 A. Kiro/Shutterstock, p.113 HasanZaidi/Shutterstock, p.114 vlalukinv/Shutterstock, p.117 Bilalstock/Shutterstock, p.117 Bo1982/Shutterstock, p.118 Harshit Srivastava S3/Shutterstock, p.119 Roselynne/Shutterstock, p.120 GaudiLab/Shutterstock, p.121 Monkey Business Images/Shutterstock, p.122 Odua Images/Shutterstock, p.123 Maja Drazic/Shutterstock, p.124 ebonyeg/ Shutterstock, p.126 legenda/Shutterstock, p.127 Rawpixel.com/Shutterstock, p.128 SpeedKingz/ Shutterstock, p.129 Pixel-Shot/Shutterstock, p.130 fizkes/Shutterstock, p.131 SLSK Photography/ Shutterstock, p.132 Aerovista Luchtfotografie/Shutterstock, p.133 fizkes/Shutterstock, p.134 Blue Planet Studio/Shutterstock, p.135 HudenDang/Shutterstock, p.136 Prathankarnpap/Shutterstock, p.136 PRILL/ Shutterstock, p.137 AnnaStills/Shutterstock, p.138 ABO PHOTOGRAPHY/Shutterstock, p.140 BearFotos/ Shutterstock, p.142 Rawpixel.com/Shutterstock, p.145 Rawpixel.com/Shutterstock, p.145 SpeedKingz/ Shutterstock, p.146 Oleg Troino/Shutterstock, p.147 Tom Wang/Shutterstock.